Making More
of Life *With* Less

Making More of Life *With* Less

SEEKING HUMILITY, SIMPLICITY, AND SILENCE

Rick Mathis, Ph.D.

Liguori/Triumph
LIGUORI, MISSOURI

Imprimi Potest:
Richard Thibodeau, C.Ss.R.
Provincial, Denver Province
The Redemptorists

Published by Liguori/Triumph
An imprint of Liguori Publications
Liguori, Missouri
www.liguori.org
www.catholicbooksonline.com

Library of Congress Cataloging-in-Publication Data

Mathis, Rick.
    Making more of life with less : seeking humility, simplicity, and silence / Rick Mathis.—1st ed.
        p. cm.
    ISBN 0-7648-1155-X (pbk.)
    1. Christian life—Catholic authors. 2. Humility—Religious aspects—Catholic Church. 3. Simplicity—Religious aspects—Catholic Church. 4. Silence—Religious aspects—Catholic Church. I. Title.

BX2350.3.M28 2004
241'.4—dc22   2003065878

The excerpt "East Coker" (page xi) is taken from *Four Quartets*, copyright 1940 by T. S. Eliot and renewed 1968 by esme Valerie Eliot. Reprinted with permission of Hartcourt, Inc.

Printed in the United States of America
08 07 06 05 04   5 4 3 2 1
First edition

Contents

Introduction

Several years ago I took a journey that changed my life. It started as a spur-of-the-moment decision. I had decided to take Friday off after a strenuous four days at work. Tensions were high as the area where I worked faced a difficult boss and impending job cuts. At first I thought that I would drive up to Nashville to visit a friend. There was something else on my mind, though.

As I considered what to do that Thursday evening, I thought about how tired I felt. It had been an eventful year. The birth of my daughter, Erica, was definitely on the plus side. Yet my work life was a disaster. I worked at an uninspiring job that really didn't suit my academic training. I blamed myself for having spent so much time getting an advanced degree only to be unable to find a job in my great love of academics. I wondered why God would give me such a desire only to have it thwarted time and again. I resigned myself to a life outside of education, but mine was not a happy resignation.

So on that Thursday evening I made a decision to visit the Abbey of Gethsemane in Kentucky. The reason

I wanted to visit this particular monastery was because it was where the famous monk and writer Thomas Merton lived before his death in 1968. The next morning I got up and made the long drive to Bardstown, Kentucky. Upon reaching Bardstown, I found the country road leading to the monastery. As I drove down the road, I felt a growing sense of apprehension. I had made no plans whatsoever for what to do at the Abbey once I arrived. I assumed that there would be an area for visitors, but I wasn't sure. I pulled into the parking lot and looked at the large structure. I saw the visitor's entrance to the side of the main building, located in a wing that appeared to be newer than the rest of the Abbey. I walked to it and opened the door. Seated at a desk was a monk clothed in the black-and-white Trappist attire I had seen in books.

"What can I do for you?" he asked.

"I was just interested in visiting the Abbey," I said wearily. "I am a Merton fan."

"That brings a lot of 'em in," he said with a smile.

"I don't suppose I could have a walk around the monastery."

"It wouldn't be a monastery if you could do that."

"Anything at all I can do around here?" I asked, thinking that I had just made a trip to do nothing more than look at the outside of a few buildings.

"Have you visited the statues? That's certainly worth doing."

"No, I haven't."

The monk directed me to follow a path down the road a ways. I thanked him and walked out the door. I proceeded down the road and found the sign to the statues.

I felt heavy as I walked. I berated myself for having driven all the way to central Kentucky without a plan. I should have thought this through. I could easily have postponed this trip and made arrangements to stay on the grounds later in the year. I knew that abbey's typically offer retreats. I also felt the burden of my worries. Why did I feel so lost when it came to a vocation? Why did meaningful work elude me? My life seemed adrift as far as work was concerned. I had to work to support my family, and saw only years of drudgery ahead. Surely God meant for me to do more.

It was a beautiful spring day as I walked alone along the path. It was much like any other wooded walkway. I wondered if Merton could have walked through these same woods, perhaps walking on this very path. After some distance I noticed a small shed to the side of the trail. I walked over to it and saw a stand within it. On the stand was a pile of papers with a rosary resting upon it. Instructions directed visitors to write down whatever concern they may have on the top sheet. Visitors were then asked to read through and pray for the concerns of the people coming to the shed before them.

I simply wrote down my need for a life of meaning and placed my paper on top of the stack. After I did this, I looked through the concerns of those who had come before me. The first, written two days before, was the one that captured my attention the most. Here a father wrote of his gravely ill young daughter. I thought how my concerns were insignificant compared to his.

I took up the rosary and prayed for this man and his daughter, along with all of the other concerns written in the shed. Finally, in spite of my weariness and a slight headache, I prayed that I might find some sense of meaning to my life.

I left the shed and started back down the trail. I must have walked for about five minutes before I came to a small break in the tree line. Patches of bright sky appeared clearly through the branches. Suddenly I felt a great sense of lightness. It was as if all of my burdens had been lifted from me. Gone was the doubt as to why I had taken this trip, as well as the concern I'd had about not having a true vocation. It was a moment of pure being.

I walked to the end of the trail and saw the statues that depicted Jesus in the Garden of Gethsemane. While the statues were impressive, they did not match my amazement at having my concerns lifted from me. I knew that future wanderers down the path would stop at that shed and pray for me. I felt that even though these prayers would happen in the future, they were already beginning to have an effect.

It has been more than twelve years since my walk. Subtle changes took place in me after that moment on the trail. I stopped thinking that the world was all about me. Slowly I released myself from the desire to lead a perfect life where all of my talents and abilities are used to maximize my good intent in the world. I realized that life is not at all about God serving me, but me serving God, wherever I may be. I came to understand the meaning of humility.

This is not to say that everything has been wonderful since then, or that I achieved anything like enlightenment. I still struggle with a great many things. I do have a basic understanding that many of my struggles result from an overinflated view of myself in the world, or from letting my fears get the best of me. It is my desire to reclaim something of my Gethsemane experience and extend it to more areas of my life that prompts me to write this book. I believe that humility, along with simplicity and silence, may contain the seeds to extending this experience.

"Humility is endless," the poet T. S. Eliot said in his poem *Four Quartets*. Looking a little more at the passage in which this statement occurs helps us to get a better understanding of what he means:

> *Do not let me hear*
> *Of the wisdom of old men, but rather their folly,*
> *Their fear of fear and frenzy, their fear of possession,*
> *Of belonging to one another, or to others, or to God*
> *The only wisdom we can hope to acquire*
> *Is the wisdom of humility: humility is endless.*

We go through our lives with our fears, many of which center upon the fear of being "discovered," of being seen for our shortcomings, real or imagined. We also fear that others will dominate us and that we will lose our freedom.

If there is any wisdom in this, it is the wisdom of humility. It is the wisdom of knowing that for all of our desire not to be controlled, we control so little. Expanding beyond Eliot's text, for all of our desire to be perfect and to lead perfect lives, the world often has something else in mind. And for all of our desire to have things turn out the way we want, they often simply don't. Humility is endless.

Is this a pessimistic realization? There is actually an

enormous amount of good in this, just as there is an enormous amount of healing. People today have gone too far in their desire to lead less-than-humble lives. Thinking that you can and should be able to control the universe leads to depression and anxiety. Things just don't bend to your will, no matter how well intentioned you may be. Believing that you must lead an affluent lifestyle also creates a lot of tension. Finally, centering your life upon what you can get rather than how you can serve creates a world of "Enron" type behavior. By this I mean a lack of concern for others and a desire only to pursue wealth and power.

Both positively and negatively, humility really is an endless virtue. We are humble when we stand before the oceans or the mountains, or look up at the stars, or in some other way consider our small selves against created nature. This can also be a positive experience when we consider the greatness of God and his love for us. We are also humble when we consider our imperfections and how doing simple things, such as exercising, losing weight, or committing to a plan to read Scripture, are often difficult for us to put into practice.

Humility contains an accurate understanding of who each of us is before God. How could we be other than humble? The Bible includes several instances of this understanding. Adam and Eve sin due to their pride in wanting to have the wisdom of God. The Psalms tell us that God deplores the proud and upholds the humble. Jesus says that the first shall be last and the last shall be first. Paul emphasizes humility on a number of occasions, most notably in pointing out that we should imitate the humility of the Son of God who humbly died on the cross for our sins. Whether we like it or not, we are *required* to be humble.

We can dwell on the negative side of this and refuse to accept humility. Yet there is a lot of good that comes out of this recognition. We have the opportunity to break out of the imprisonment of perfection and the desire to control. We can stop thinking that everything will always turn out our way, and stop bemoaning our circumstances when they don't. Humility opens us to that great but momentary lightness and joy that I experienced on the grounds of the Abbey of Gethsemane.

Humility is truly an endless virtue. It is endless to the extent that it tells us so much about who we are. It also provides endless graces if practiced well. Simplicity and silence are endless virtues for much the same reasons. This is because these three "virtues" are really related to one another. To be humble is not to live a lavish lifestyle filled with all of the complexities that typically go along with such a life. To be humble is to seek simplicity. It is to find ways of living that are more akin to service rather than to gain. Silence, too, is related to humility. How many times do we speak out of pride, hoping that somehow we will make ourselves look good while making others look bad? How many times do we slander others out of a sense of moral pride? "Silence is golden" as the old saying goes. By taking silence to mean not total silence, but rather restraint in speech, to be selectively silent, we understand how such a humble virtue provides endless benefit.

Readers of contemporary religious writing will notice that humility, simplicity, and silence relate to the monastic tradition. Monks and nuns take vows of poverty, chastity, and obedience. Underscoring these vows are humility, simplicity, and silence. Monks in the Christian tradition are asked to lead humble and simple lives characterized by periodic silence. Such a life, it is thought, helps to transcend the bounds of ego so that individuals may better understand and practice the will of God.

Many popular books focus specifically upon monastic ideas and practices. The phenomenal success of Kathleen Norris' *The Cloister Walk* shows that there is a real interest here. Many are striving for a holier life, and feel that monasticism has something to offer such a life, even if one never intends to enter an abbey.

In writing about humility, simplicity, and silence, I am obviously influenced by such writers as Kathleen Norris and Thomas Merton. But I also want to look at these from other perspectives as well. Humility is a virtue that is not only encouraged by monasticism but is also a fundamental part of the Bible. How do we reconcile this with a world that often looks down upon the humble? There has been a growing interest in simplicity over the last twenty years or so. The interest comes as much from an interest in ecology and a reaction against consumerism than it does from anything else. How do we live simply in a world of increasing hours at work and seemingly endless external activities? Silence is perhaps the most difficult to separate from monasticism. What other tradition or institution would encourage people to be silent? Yet overcommunication is a real problem in our world. Television and movies provide troubling messages, messages that do more harm than good. Is there a way to silence these? People, too, fail to pay attention to the harm that their words do. Some also fail to appreciate how their words belie a prideful spirit. Is there a way to be silent when the world views the quiet soul with either suspicion or condescension? To be silent is also to allow time for really listening to what others have to say. Is there a way to learn silence when we forever desire to express our opinions?

This book explores the thinking behind humility, simplicity, and silence. It also looks at how each of these may be applied to daily life. Each topic will be dealt with in three chapters. The chapters will stimulate thinking about the topic by discussing some aspect of it. The approach will at times be practical, at times theoretical, and at times unconventional. The idea is to look at each virtue from different angles. The final chapter ties all of the previous chapters together and looks specifically at how to put the ideas together into a more joyous life. I could have titled this book "Endless Joy," because I believe that humility, simplicity, and silence point the way to joyful living. Jesus said that the key to eternal life is through loving God and loving your neighbor as yourself. I believe that we experience something of this life now and that it is characterized by joy. In humility we learn to serve God and one another. This is the best way of showing our love. Simplicity and silence, too, enable us better to listen to and love God and others. These virtues, springing as they do from a love of God, are the source of joy.

Expanding the Moment

I said earlier that I was interested in expanding the momentary feeling of lightness and joy that I experienced on the way to the statues. I need to comment a little more on why I feel that humility, simplicity, and silence may contribute to expanding this moment. Much has been written in popular literature about fear being the factor that keeps people from experiencing bliss. *A Course in Miracles* and the numerous books inspired by it emphasize that fear is an illusion and that recognizing this fact frees us from it. This truth is actually found in the Bible. One of the main messages of 1 John is that God is perfect love and that perfect love drives out fear.

So why not focus on fear in this book? For one, there are already so many books on this topic that it hardly adds to anything to write another book about it. But more than that, I believe that the three virtues we will be looking at are actually another method of experiencing God's perfect love and getting past the fear that often grips us in daily life. By this I mean the fear we have that something bad will happen, or that someone or something is threatening our present or future, or that the future will not turn out as we would like.

When practiced well, humility challenges both our sense of importance and our need to constantly defend ourselves. Simplicity challenges the need to be always acquiring things, as well as the fear that if we don't give in to our ambition then we will miss out on something important. Silence involves both outer silence and inner silence. Outer silence releases us from the fear that we may not sound impressive to someone, perhaps someone in power. It allows us to listen to and love others. Inner silence enables us to shut down the constant stream of things we tell ourselves. It creates the space we need to be able to draw from the deep well of an experience with God. How can we really listen to and experience God when we are constantly talking to ourselves? Many times it is the fear of things past, present, and future that keeps us from having this experience.

I know these things all to well because I am constantly in situations that create stress and fear. As someone who works in a healthcare related field, I understand and experience the apprehensions that go along with being in a rapidly changing industry. As a manager, I understand the pressures that are a part of supervising others, as well as the fear of knowing that some of my decisions will backfire on me. As a parent, I face the anxieties that accompany trying to protect my children while at the same time giving them enough freedom so that they can live a normal life. As a Christian, I worry that perhaps I have not done enough to make the world a better place. I worry that I have not been very good at loving God and loving others.

As a result of all of these pressures, it is quite easy to feel exhausted, unspiritual, and troubled at the end of a long day. My Gethsemane experience haunts me. I want more of it, and I want others to enjoy the same experience. I want to stop the excuses I make to myself that I can't have more of this experience because of all the pressures I am under. I also want to stop telling myself that I would be more loving and caring toward others if only my circumstances were better.

I suspect the situations that you face are not much different than mine. With this in mind, we will walk down this path together. Together we will see how humility, simplicity, and silence are an effective antidote against the fears that often grip us. We will also see how each contains seeds of a true experience of God. We know that we are close to God when we experience great joy and are able to reflect this joy to others.

"Humility is endless," as Eliot wrote. Let's begin our walk together by looking at this first endless virtue.

ONE

It's Okay to Be Humble

A few years ago I attended the twentieth anniversary of my high-school reunion. I surprised myself by going, if such a thing is possible, as I was never particularly popular or happy in high school. Yet go I did, giving no small amount of thought to what I would wear to the event. I attended a large suburban school during a time when long hair and jeans were the predominant style. I put on a modest jacket and tie, thinking that I would be grossly overdressed for the occasion. Imagine my surprise when I showed up at the hotel ballroom and was confronted by several people in expensive suits and dresses. Former nonconformists were eager to show that they had "made it" and that they could afford to spend their earnings on expensive clothes. Humbled by my modest attire, I found myself yet again out of step with my old high-school crowd.

Humility is not something that is encouraged by society or by popular culture. Far from it! Instead, we are encouraged to be achievers and consumers. The message is not to serve one another by putting yourself last, but to "walk with the giants," to quote the title from a popular self-help book. Happiness, wealth, and success, it is argued, are there for the taking, provided you apply just the right strategy and the right mental attitude.

But there is another side to this. While we are encouraged to attain high social status and to consume, there are other elements at work. Books with such titles as *Voluntary Simplicity* and *Your Money or Your Life* are growing in popularity. We also hear such things as "those who strive to climb the ladder of success often find it leaning against the wrong wall." Finally, we read of the health benefits of volunteerism and service to others. We don't hear the same being said of extreme ambition. It is almost assumed that people focused solely on achievement and power will suffer either physical or emotional breakdown at some point in their lives.

What is going on here? If you take these opposing ideas seriously, and add a twist of Dickens, it looks as if we are living in both the proudest of times and the humblest of times. People nowadays are encouraged to achieve while at the same time the price of achievement is documented and well understood. Perhaps such schizophrenic thinking is at least partially responsible for the increases in depression and the prescription of antidepressants. We live within the horns of a dilemma. Should we seek wealth and power and risk poor health and a loss of self, or should we seek humility and simplicity and risk being out of step with society (and our former classmates)?

Based upon my observations at my high school reunion and elsewhere, I'd say that the urge to achieve is winning this battle. The constant stream of advertising and the desire for more and more keeps us looking for the next computer upgrade and thinking of buying the bigger house, or at least making the "needed" renovation. As such, we individually and collectively sink deeper into debt and must lead complicated, tension-filled lives if we hope to escape from this debt.

As we begin to consider humility, it is important to understand this situation. In many respects, humility is a forgotten virtue. It has been eclipsed by our achievement-oriented culture. To tell people that you are trying to be more humble is likely to raise an eyebrow. They may either misunderstand you or think that you are joking in some way.

Is it okay to be humble? The fact is that like any other virtue, humility can be done poorly. The first thing that might come to mind when thinking about humility is the image of a weak and generally servile person. Always seeking not to offend, such a person has a hard time expressing her opinions and is constantly averting her eyes. An inveterate follower, a humble individual might get caught up in some unfortunate movement or might fail to speak out against injustice. After all, being humble means humility in having and expressing an opinion, doesn't it?

The second image that comes to mind is the person who is falsely humble. We all have had experience with this type of individual. This is the person who really is good at something, but is constantly downplaying his talent. In his book, *Wishful Thinking,* Frederick Buechner characterizes this person in the following way:

Humility is often confused with the gentlemanly self-deprecation of saying you're not much of a bridge player when you know perfectly well you are. Conscious or otherwise, this kind of humility is a form of gamesmanship. If you really *aren't* much of a bridge player, you're apt to be rather proud of yourself for admitting it so humbly. This kind of humility is a form of low comedy.

A variation of this is the person who is constantly putting himself last, but only to the extent that everyone can see it. Such a person may feel that he is scoring metaphysical points through his humble efforts being noticed both here and in the hereafter. The problem with such a person is that it is not humility he is practicing so much as a suppressed form of pride.

The third negative image of humility is that of the chronic underachiever. This is the person who may have a lot of ability, but fails to use it due to a negative self-image. This image could come from any number of places. It might be from something in her background. Or, it could be the acceptance of negative views of people and things with which such a person in associated. Rather than taking pride in her cultural background, for example, such a person might use it as an excuse not to achieve. A sense of less than stellar origins or background keeps such a person from achieving whatever goals she may have in mind.

Defending Humility

Let's look at these negative views of humility in order. Does humility require a weak and servile attitude? I believe that this is really a perversion of the virtue. There are a couple of ways of arguing against this. As we know from Aristotle, virtue is a mean. Aristotle looked at courage and pointed out that the soldier who rushes headlong into an enemy force is not courageous but foolhardy. On the other hand, the soldier who shrinks from battle is cowardly. The courageous soldier is one who acts between these two extremes. This person uses discretion and wisdom along with valor in displaying courage.

The same is true of humility. An obsequious and servile person is just that, obsequious and servile. A boastful and overly proud person is the opposite of such an individual. This is the person who can't do anything without reminding you of how great and wonderful he or she is. Humility is somewhere in between. Humility doesn't mean worshiping at the feet of another. Nor is it in the person who wishes to sing to the world about his accomplishments. It is the person who uses discretion and wisdom in practicing humility.

The Scriptures give us an opportunity to refine this view of humility a little more sharply. We know that Jesus charged us to be humble in saying that the first shall be last and the last shall be first. Even in his immediate environment we know he often upbraided his disciples for their concern with who was the most important among them. Paul, too, often charged Christians to be humble and to serve one another.

Although telling us to be humble, Jesus' life shows us that he was not humble in the extreme, servile sense of the term. When he saw injustice, he did something about it. We hear of him throwing the moneychangers out of the Temple, which is hardly the act of a servile or weak individual. Nor did Jesus follow the laws of the day that forbade healing on the Sabbath. Far from being timid and giving in to authority, Jesus was ready to challenge practices he knew were wrong.

The same can certainly be said for Paul. Paul was famous for sharing his opinions about all kinds of issues. Moreover, he was quick to criticize behavior that was inconsistent with Christian living. He goes so far as to warn followers about individuals whom he felt were disruptive to the faith. Paul was hardly a man whom one could characterize as being afraid to share his opinion.

The humility of Jesus and Paul does not get in the way of what I think of as spiritual assertiveness. By this I mean working positively to ensure that God's kingdom is being expanded. Such expansion is prevented by unjust practices or by activities that harm people in some way. So while humility means refraining from boasting and being last, it does not require passively accepting whatever happens to be going on in society. Laws and practices that either create suffering or prevent the healing of this suffering must be questioned and, if necessary, broken. Individuals who cause pain to others must be opposed. Humility does not ask that a wife stay with an abusive husband anymore than it asks an individual to support a corrupt institution or practice.

When you consider that humility involves first and foremost humble service to God, it really points to a very active lifestyle. That is why Jesus and Paul both emphasized humility while at the same time acting and speaking against the wrongful practices they confronted. In serving God, Jesus and Paul could not tolerate the ungodly practices they confronted.

One modern example of such humble service that comes to mind is Robert F. Kennedy. Bobby Kennedy was known as a crusader of sorts. Whether one agrees with his politics or not, it is certainly true that he acted out of the kind of humble service that I describe above. The words that his brother Edward spoke at his funeral perhaps sum up the active call of humble living. His brother asked that Bobby be remembered "simply as a good and decent man, who saw wrong and tried to right it, saw suffering and tried to heal it, saw war and tried to stop it." I can think of no more fitting description of the active life to which Christian humility calls us.

The other negative view of humility is that of the person who is really falsely humble. This is the person who may actually be quite proficient at something, but who constantly makes self-deprecating comments, often to the point of irritation. Buechner's example of a good bridge player is as good as any. Such comments are, as Buechner indicates, forms of gamesmanship and low comedy. Generally such humility puts the intelligent listener on notice that a trick is about to be played or some subtle form of manipulation is taking place. At a minimum, it appears that the falsely humble person is trying to keep herself from getting ensnared in the trap of pride. But the problem is that self-deprecating comments really show that the trap is already sprung and the speaker is already caught.

Buechner identifies the way out of this unfortunate practice. He writes that true humility doesn't consist of thinking ill of yourself, "but of not thinking of yourself much differently from the way you'd be apt to think of anybody else. It is the capacity for being no more and no less pleased when you play your own hand well than when your opponents do." Humility requires a certain detachment that involves not a deprecating focus, but not much of a focus at all. This releases you to serve God and others.

The third concern with humility is that it appears inconsistent with certain ideas of pride that we take to be healthy in our society. Not being proud of yourself and your accomplishments can lead to dysfunctional behavior. On a broader, social level, pride in your cultural background is certainly an important attitude to have when you are part of a group that has suffered from discrimination in one form or another. It allows a kind of healing to take place.

Does it go against humility to be proud of either your accomplishments or a group of people with whom you identify? For example, if I were able to earn a degree of higher learning in spite of coming from an impoverished background, wouldn't it be okay to be proud of that? If I were proud, would that go against Jesus and Paul's statements encouraging humility?

Going back to Aristotle's idea of a mean is helpful here. Humility doesn't require a constant putting down of one's self. It wouldn't help to say, "Yes I've got a college degree, but that is really nothing, especially since I am an imperfect person." Nor would it help for someone to be boastful about his accomplishments. Humility is more akin to Buechner's idea of not thinking much of yourself at all. It would certainly be okay to think well of yourself for getting a degree in spite of the odds. But a good, spiritually based practice of humility would ask that you be wary of going too far; that is, of focusing so much upon yourself and your accomplishments that you lose focus on everything else.

This gets us back to expanding God's kingdom. You need to have a certain amount of self-esteem in order to work for this kingdom. This esteem can come from the understanding that we are children of God and that God loves us. This realization doesn't fit with an overly negative self-image. Moreover, such an image really gets in the way because it still contains the conceited view that you should be the focus rather than God. Falling into the trap of constantly singing your laurels doesn't help either. This also puts you at the center rather than God. In either case it is not God's kingdom that is being expanded, but your own. The path to humility is opened when you stop looking at yourself either positively or negatively and start looking at God.

But what about Black Pride, Native American Pride, and the other sorts of "Pride" movements that are so popular? Again, to the extent that these allow healing to take place, these are good movements. These efforts encourage healthy self-esteem. From a spiritual perspective, the trick is not to become so proud that you lose your focus upon serving God. If you become consumed with whatever pride movement you may be a part of, then you may lose sight of the fact that we are all God's children. In other words, too much of a good thing is still too much.

Humility does not have to be associated with servile, passive behavior. Nor should it be identified with a false, self-deprecating lifestyle. Finally, it should not be associated with the failure to achieve due to something in a person's background. All such examples are really perversions of humility.

Humble Pride

What, then, is humility? When it comes down to it, humility is really the ability to focus less on yourself and more on God. This, again, need not be done in a negative way. It does not mean that you have to deny yourself or engage in various forms of self-flagellation in order to destroy your ego. The problem with such practices is that they only make you focus on yourself all the more. Instead, you simply need to realize that the universe is not about you so much as it is about you serving God. How do you do that? You do that by being a reflection of God's love to others.

Sometimes such ideas are best captured by an oxymoron. That is, through putting together two opposite words. Humble pride is such a phrase. If you take seriously the idea that virtue is a mean, then it may well be that humility and pride are two ideas that need each other. The excesses of each contribute to the idea of a moderate and good practice of both. From this comes the idea of "humble pride." Interestingly, monk and writer Brother David Steindl-Rast hit upon this idea in defining humility in his book *Gratefulness, the Heart of Prayer*. Like Buechner, he is concerned with the idea of feigned humility:

Many people think that humility is a pious lie committed by people who claim to be worse than they know themselves to be, so that they can secretly pride themselves in being so humble. In truth, however, to be humble simply means to be earthy. The word "humble" is related to "humus," the vegetable mold of top soil. It is also related to human and humor. If we accept and embrace the earthiness of our human condition (and a bit of humor helps) we shall find ourselves doing so with humble pride.

Steindl-Rast's idea of humble pride goes back to the recognition of who we are. Accepting our humanity for its entire "earthiness" allows us to embrace both humility and pride. We can be humble in our recognition of our fallibility and our less than perfect natures. This recognition can take place without a sense of anger or angst. In fact, it can even be a humorous recognition, as well as a recognition that gets us out of serving ourselves and into serving God.

There is another definition in Steindl-Rast's book that is helpful in understanding and practicing humble pride. This is his definition of Zero.

The very shape of zero, written as 0, expresses emptiness. But the full circle also signifies fullness. Zero stands for nothing, but by adding zero to a number we can multiply it tenfold, a hundredfold, a thousandfold. Gratefulness gives fullness to life by adding nothing. Understanding 0 by becoming 0—that's what gratefulness is all about.

Humility and 0 are, of course, closely linked. Humility is all about not thinking so much about ourselves. It is about emptying ourselves so that we may become filled with God. When we empty ourselves through humility, we allow ourselves to become so much more than we as individuals are alone. That is, of course, a great source of positive pride.

The fact is that the practice of humble pride is really enormously transformational. It keeps us focused in the right direction. If you are too proud, then you are deeply focused upon yourself. You are always thinking about your accomplishments or the accomplishments of those around you. You are forever boastful about these.

Yet the same focus is contained within an overly humble attitude. Here you also end up thinking only of yourself. You are focused upon your shortcomings and your unworthiness. A good acid test is this: Anytime you focus exclusively upon yourself, whether negatively or positively, you run the risk of losing your focus upon God.

Being zero is a good way of letting go of either an overly negative or an overly positive view of yourself. Being zero is a way of not thinking much of yourself at all. It creates an emptiness that is filled with the love of God. Such a practice of humility can't help but be transformational.

If humility is about being zero, it is also about putting yourself and your actions in service to God. This means placing your actions in service to others as well. This does not mean, as you might suppose, that you have to sell everything you own and take up missionary work in some impoverished country. As noble as such activities are, most people simply aren't going to do this. You can start to be humble instead by performing literally thousands of small acts right where you are. It means seeing your work, whatever it may be, against the broader context of building God's kingdom. What can you do to encourage your employer to better serve your community? How can you better serve the people in your immediate environment? "Do small things with great love" is something that Mother Teresa said. The idea, I believe, is to take on the attitude of loving service to the people around you. Just taking on that attitude, here and now, is part of the transformation.

Please understand, too, that practicing this type of humility at work or anywhere else for that matter does not translate into excessive toleration. Humility doesn't mean that you must let difficult people have their way. I have had to become aware of this as the result of being a manager. In such a capacity, there are certain behaviors that just get in the way of teamwork and prevent people from making good contributions at work. You might think that humility would make someone think that he really can't deal with disruptive or troubling people. Who am I, after all, to say anything? True humility means dealing with such people head on. It means giving people feedback and telling them how what they are doing is creating problems for others. If they continue to create such problems, it means removing them from the environment. In such instances humility is not always easy. It is, however, the right thing to do.

Is it okay to be humble? I hope by now that I have convinced you that it is. Perhaps now the idea that the first shall be last and the last first is a little clearer. Those who are constantly trying to put themselves ahead of everyone else end up with a pointless life. They serve their own ego, which is to say that they don't serve much at all. Those who put themselves last end up being first in that they find the great joy involved with serving God and others. Such people find that in being last they experience the unspeakable presence of God and are able to reflect this presence to others. They become builders of the kingdom of God.

As you attend the reunions and other events that make up the rest of your life, you are likely to see that living humbly, that living last, often isn't encouraged. Instead you will see that people will continually be showing off their fine clothes and talking about everything from private school educations for their children to the late model car they are driving. The "one with the most toys wins" mentality is hard to get around in our society. It's hard to keep from getting caught up in this way of thinking. I find myself there from time to time.

Yet there is a better way. There is a way that doesn't require you to berate yourself for your imperfections anymore than it doesn't call on you to boast about whatever thing in your life you feel is praiseworthy. More importantly, this way calls you to healing and to action in service to God. The way I am talking about is humility. Sometimes you need to tell yourself that it's okay to be humble. Then you need to give it a try.

Returning to my experience at the Abbey of Gethsemane, you might wonder how practicing humility expands the lightness and joy I felt there. In any given week I am subject to fears that keep me from having such experiences. I make decisions that end up having less than ideal consequences. At times others are quick to criticize these decisions, making me feel even worse. I deal with people who think I don't know what I am doing, and sometimes they make me think they are right.

Humility is strong medicine against such feelings. Of course I don't have perfect knowledge about outcomes. Does anyone? Of course not everyone I encounter in life will like me and appreciate me for what I am. Is anyone so fortunate? How prideful of me to think that everything I do in life will work and that all of the significant people in my life will think I'm just wonderful. When I remember this, and mix in a little prayer, something great happens, something not unlike my Gethsemane experience. I'm freed.

TWO

Endless Healing

J ohn got a call around 5:30 Tuesday evening. He could tell something was wrong the minute he picked up the phone.

"What are you doing home?" his father, Dan, asked, his voice a little slurred.

"I'm always home at this time," John said.

The next voice John heard was that of his Uncle Allen. He remembered that his aunt and uncle had come up from Atlanta to spend a few days with his father.

"I think you'd better get over here," Allen said. "Something is wrong with your father."

John's mind raced as he drove the twenty miles to his father's apartment. He wondered what was wrong. If it were serious, how was he going to take care of his father? Dan was a widower in his mid seventies. The victim of a mild heart attack some years before, he wasn't in great shape, but up until now he wasn't in bad shape either.

John's suspicions were confirmed when he walked through the door to his father's apartment. He had a little medical knowledge from a brief flirtation with going into medicine. Based upon the information he was able to glean over the phone, he guessed that his father had suffered from a stroke. He was able to get Dan out the door of his apartment with a little prodding and pleading. Along the way he discovered that the symptoms had started early that morning, well before his aunt and uncle arrived. Even then, Dan asked them not to contact John. He didn't want to bother him. According to his uncle, however, Dan was having a hard time walking and seemed disoriented. They finally convinced Dan to push the speed dial button for John's telephone number.

John knew that it is essential to get a stroke victim to the hospital as soon as possible. There is a good chance that aggressive treatment can help someone during the early stages of a stroke. He rushed his father to the hospital, but guessed that the time for this therapy had passed. He soon discovered that he was right. Dan's stroke had begun several hours before. The time for aggressive therapy had passed.

John was very hard on himself as he sat by the bedside of his father. Why hadn't he called his father that morning? He should have had a pattern of doing that. Instead he let himself get caught up in his own life. He forgot that he had a father with a heart condition who probably should be checked on daily. His "busyness" kept Dan from calling him. After all, his father said he didn't call because he didn't want to bother John.

This was just the beginning of John's guilt. An only son, he had primary responsibility for Dan. But there was no possibility of his being able to take him into his home. John's wife, Julia, had never really clicked with Dan. The fact that John and Julia had two small children didn't

help either. John did not know what his father's progno-
sis was, but he was sure that he had a long road ahead of
him in terms of recovery and rehabilitation. He had discussed the possibility of long-term care with his father,
but he wasn't sure if he had enough of the details in
place to make the transition smoothly. In the midst of
worrying about his father's health, and engaging in self-
criticism for not checking on him more often, he also
blamed himself for not having enough of the details in
place to deal with his father's long-term illness.

Beyond Blame

Many of us will face situations such as this in our lives.
Events come out of the blue, and we take personal responsibility for them, often to troubling and unhealthy
degrees. John's reaction to his father's stroke is probably
as common a reaction as you will get when it comes to
caring for loved ones. When someone in our family is
hurt or injured, we wonder if we could have done something differently to keep it from happening or at least
make it less catastrophic. And, of course, if we had perfect knowledge, we probably could. If John had known
his father was going to have a stroke, he could have made
a point of being there the minute it happened. But he
could only act on the information he had. What he knew
was that his father was in fairly good health and had
recovered well from a previous heart attack. The possibility of a stroke hadn't even occurred to John.

The same is true of Dan's healthcare. John had taken
the rudimentary steps of having a plan in place should a
health crisis occur in his father's life. He made sure that

his father had adequate healthcare coverage and he knew where the closest hospital was. He had even helped his father purchase a long-term care policy. Again, if he had known that his father was going to have a stroke exactly when he did, then he could have done even more. But John assumed that such an event was years into the future.

What does humility have to do with these types of situations? The above shows the kinds of doubts and recriminations that go through many people's minds when they face a difficult situation. I don't believe that humility can eradicate the initial misgivings that take place in such a situation. I think a lot of that is just hard wired into the emotional systems of many people. When something bad happens we seem naturally inclined to engage in "if only I had done something differently" thinking.

I do believe that humility helps to shorten the amount of time it takes to end the negative thinking that takes place. It may also lessen the severity of the self-criticism. It certainly helps with getting on with life after such an event has taken place. This is extremely important in a situation such as John's. He is going to need to make a lot of key decisions about his father's care after the stroke. It will be hard for him to do this if his mind is clouded with a lot of emotional doubts and misgivings. He needs to be thinking clearly so that he can make decisions that are in the best interests of everyone involved. He can't do this if he is engaged in self-criticism.

Humility is a salve for such situations. It helps people to realize that they don't have perfect knowledge. No one can be expected to have perfect knowledge as to what will happen. Nor can anyone expect to have a plan in place to address all of the adverse events that can happen in a lifetime.

These facts are consistent of some of the basic tenants of cognitive psychology. This branch of psychology has proven effective in dealing with such problems as depression and anger. People often get depressed and angry because they are thinking irrationally. They may get depressed because something didn't go their way, or because some significant person or persons in their lives do not like them. They may get angry for the same reasons. An effective treatment for such situations is to ask yourself a few questions. Is it really rational to suppose that every person you meet will like you and respond positively to you? Is it rational to think that everything you try will have spectacular results? The answer to both questions, of course, is no.

Humility makes the same points and can also lead to mental health and healing. Humility asks that we stop thinking that we are somehow perfect or all-knowing. It reminds us that people will not always like us and that things will happen for which we are ill prepared. In modern terms we can think of humility as the ultimate reality check. Without it we would be doomed to endless cycles of self-criticism.

Like cognitive therapy, humility helps us to deal with the world in a healthier fashion. It heals us from negative and self-destructive thinking. You might fear, however, that it leads to apathy. If you know that you are imperfect, then why try to be good, ethical, or successful at anything? Why not just give up trying? The fact is that humility may be used to justify a person's laziness. Again, the idea is to see humility as a mean. People who are prone to laziness and a lack of concern shouldn't justify this under the guise of humility. They aren't being humble as much as they are being irresponsible. Instead, humility is a way for people who tend to take too much responsibility for life's difficulties to question such unhealthy tendencies. As is true of all medicines, humility works for some conditions (such as perfectionism) but is detrimental to others (such as laziness and apathy).

Humility not only heals the emotional tendencies many have toward self-blame but it also helps to heal relationships. The acceptance of your own imperfection may make you more understanding when you encounter it in others. Such an understanding often leads to forgiveness, which is the primary means of healing broken relationships. We often set high expectations for the people around us, and can be quick to condemn them when they don't live up to those expectations. Humility helps us to understand that just as we aren't perfect, others aren't perfect either. We therefore need to think carefully before being overly critical of others.

I believe such thinking is behind the biblical advice to practice forgiveness and refrain from judgment. Once we realize that we are not perfect, we can lessen our criticism of others. We understand that while others have their faults, we have our own faults as well. We can use this understanding to heal our relationships with people whom we have judged harshly. We can even use it to check our tendencies to judgment before they take place. Humility becomes a preventative treatment for unhealthy relationships. It keeps us from giving in to our tendencies to judge others and to be in unhealthy relationships with them.

We have talked about humility in terms of healing self-criticism and leading to the forgiveness of others. We know that ending self-criticism and practicing forgiveness leads to overall improved health. There is another way that humility heals. Humility, we know, is all about service. It is about putting aside your self-concern so that you can help others. Jesus is our model here. Although fully Divine, he took on the role of a servant and died a humble death so that we might live.

Humble service certainly contributes to the healing of others. Humility can be very much a part of taking on such tasks as visiting the sick, tending to the poor, and helping those who are in otherwise unfortunate circumstances. These activities are part of setting aside time that you could be spending on some pleasurable pursuit and spending it helping others instead. This, of course, is very helpful and healing toward the person or persons whom you are helping.

Such activities not only heal the people that are helped, however. They also heal the helper. Dr. Dean Ornish and others are exploring how altruistic behaviors actually have a healing impact upon the people engaging in the altruism. It is as if such people participate in a great healing project in which everyone benefits. What we are discovering is that people who help others end up being healthier and happier themselves. So the proud person who feels too important to spend time with those in need ends up less healthy than the humble individual who engages in acts of service to others.

Let's sum up all of the ways in which humility heals before discussing how to put them into practice. We have seen that humility combats tendencies to unhealthy

perfectionism and self-criticism. Such thinking often para-
lyzes us. Instead of constructive action, we shut down
while we blame ourselves for not having predicted some
unfortunate event. Humility enables us to realize that
we are imperfect in both our knowledge or in our actions. It heals us so that we can get on with our lives and
make the decisions necessary to cope with whatever situation may be facing us.

Humility also heals with respect to relationships. Realizing that we are imperfect ought to help us to understand that others aren't perfect as well. It opens the door
to forgiveness and helps to prevent our thinking negatively about others. It heals the wounds caused by disap-
pointment and anger. Moreover, it can keep such wounds
from ever taking place.

Finally, humility leads to healing service. If I can put
aside my concern with myself and, in humility, begin to
think of others, then I am more likely to engage in altruistic acts. Such acts not only help heal the people in need,
but they have positive health consequences upon the
person offering the service. It is as if everyone involved
gets to participate in the great dance of healing.

Overcoming the Difficulties

Although all of this makes sense, it is worth asking why
it is often difficult to put these ideas into practice. Let's
take a look at each one of the areas of humble healing to
see where the problems are. The idea of applying humility to self-criticism is one that is particularly difficult.
Although humility is easy to grasp on an intellectual level,
it is often difficult to accept on an emotional one. There

is nothing like that feeling in the pit of your stomach when something bad has happened and you feel that it is the result of something you should or should not have done.

The best way of coping with this is to understand worrisome events as a kind of trauma that happens to the body. When a bad event takes place for which you feel responsible, just let the experience of blame happen. Realize while it is going on, however, that this is really a natural process from which you will eventually heal. At some point your reason is going to take over and you will be able to cope with the situation better. You will be able to remind yourself that not everything is your fault and that you can't anticipate every unfortunate event.

It also helps to understand your individual tendencies so that you can better find means of coping with self-criticism. I have heard it said that most people have the majority of their issues in one of three areas. These are with control, acceptance, and security. So when faced with making decisions regarding the health of a loved one, some may feel concerned that they are losing control as a result of the situation. They may feel frustrated because they cannot take total control of the situation but must rely on the decisions of the professionals involved.

Others may feel that their decisions with respect to their loved one may result in their being judged as unacceptable by others. They may be so concerned about the judgment of others that they are unable to act effectively in the situation. Rather than assessing for his or her self what should be done, such an individual will be trying to satisfy the opinions of others.

Still a third group worries about their own sense of security. Dealing with the illness of another may make them reflect to a great extent upon their own mortality. Such a person may focus upon their own health and well-being rather than those of the person in need. Their lack of security makes it difficult for them to think clearly.

Understanding which of the three areas you have a tendency to fall into helps when you are in a traumatic situation. If you have control issues, for example, then you can recognize these for what they are as they arise. This helps in moving beyond recovery and into the action phase. The same is true of security and acceptance. Knowing that an event is going to make you feel insecure, or that whatever action you take as a result may be criticized, helps you to put some distance between yourself and your emotions. This both heals and enables action.

Healing relationships with others is also a very difficult task. We all have relationships that are less-than-perfect. These may be people with whom we work or relatives that just seem to irritate us in one way or another. Humility helps us to understand not only the imperfections of others, but our own imperfections in finding effective ways of dealing with others.

This latter realization helps you to cope with situations where you simply may not be able to find a way of dealing with a particular person. This may be a person who has harmed you in some way, or whom you perceive is not acting in your best interests. Rather than beating your head against the wall wondering how you can get along with such an individual, it sometimes helps humbly to realize that there is simply nothing you can do. Realize that this may just be someone with whom you just cannot interact with and feel good about it. This is not to say that you should hate such a person or work against him or her. Instead, simply pray for this person, while realizing that you don't necessarily have to reconcile fully either. In all humility, leave such a person to God and get on with your life. That is probably the most healing thing that you can do.

The service aspects of humility present another difficulty in times as busy and complex as our own. It is often hard to make the time to be of service to others. This is particularly true if you have a lot of family responsibilities. You may feel that you need to work in order to provide for your family, and that you need to spend the rest of your time attending more directly to their needs. This can include cooking for them and taking them to various activities. At the end of the day, there simply isn't enough time to work with the homeless or otherwise care for the needy.

Anne Lemonte in her book *Traveling Mercies* gives us an image to help to deal with such situations. She says that we are all like people in a physician's waiting room waiting to see the great healer. While we are here the best we can do is to help as much as possible the other people who are waiting with us. I like this image for a variety of reasons. It points out that no matter what your condition may be, you can always help someone else who is equally or even more distressed. So while you may be in the waiting room dealing with your own illness, you can still pay attention to your surroundings and look for opportunities to help others.

Another reason I like this image is that it shows how

you can help people where you are. You don't have to travel to a Third World country to be of service. Life will give you plenty of opportunities to help those just outside your doorstep. While you may be ailing in certain areas of your life at the moment, you can also keep your eyes open to those who may be ailing around you. Knowing that, in the end, we will see the great Healer, you can apply your healing service to ease the suffering of others.

Remember, too, that whatever situation you may happen to find yourself in will change. Your children will grow older and your time constraints will alter. Instead of spending more time at the office or at social gatherings, consider spending more time directly helping others. In so doing you not only help them, you help yourself as well. Be a humble healer rather than an active accumulator of possessions.

I'd like to summarize all of this by returning to the story of John. We left John in a state of self-criticism and self-recrimination. He hated that he had not better anticipated his father's stroke and that he was not there for him when it took place. He can use the ideas above to get beyond this negative thinking and begin to take more positive steps to deal with the situation. He can overcome his self-loathing with a strong dose of rationality and humility. Of course he hadn't anticipated his father's health problem. Who could have? And even if he had been in the habit of calling his father every day, how could he have known to call at the precise time that would have made a difference?

Humility can also help heal relationship problems that John may experience as a result of his father's stroke.

John may blame others for the situation. He may even blame his father for failing to get in touch with him sooner. Humility helps John to realize that people aren't all-knowing and that they often make mistakes. Spending a lot of time blaming others for what happens tends to hamper rather than help the healing process.

John can also put the service aspect of humility to good use. Undoubtedly John will be a large part of whatever future care his father will need. He can either see this as a burden or as a grace. Humility will help him to deal with the limitations that he feels caring for his father may place upon him. He can learn to put some of his own needs aside as he attends to those of his father. Again, humility does not require that Dan leave his family and spend all of his time caring for his father. It does require that he ensure that his father is well cared for, and that he balance the needs of the other people in his life with those of Dan's. The fact is that humility will help him to achieve this balance with a sense of joy and grace.

There is an even deeper sense in which humble service is helpful. John is likely to find that as a result of his father's stroke he is going to find more people in need cross his path. He will find this at the hospital where Dan is cared for as well as in the rehabilitation activities that take place after the hospital stay. John can use this as an opportunity to find ways of helping and healing the other people with health problems that he comes across. He can be a source of comfort and grace to others.

As it turns out, John placed his father into an assisted living facility that his father liked. There John could see that his father was well cared for and got the treatment he needed. This also allowed Dan a certain measure of independence. John began spending time doing volunteer work at the facility, and experienced the joys of humble healing firsthand. He also found that this healed his life in other ways. He began to experience a sense of grace and became less concerned with having all the details of his life worked out to the nth degree.

Humility is truly an endless virtue. It also provides for endless healing. In putting aside a proud concern for yourself, you begin to experience the joy of caring for others. Not only are you healed, but you also become a healer. This makes all of the difference.

THREE

Humble Climbing

Most of us have had experiences of feeling either close to or far away from God. Sometimes it's hard to explain why we feel that way. A feeling of closeness may simply be a grace, while a feeling of distance may be the result of some other mysterious factor. Sometimes, however, our feelings of proximity are easy to understand. Feeling close to God can result from performing some benevolent act or doing something that we know to be consistent with his will. Distance results from doing things that we know are either wrong or outside of his will for us.

Medieval thinkers, such as Saint Benedict, translated the idea of living according to God's will into the metaphor of a ladder. The steps of the ladder represent disciplines that we are to follow in order to be closer to God. Failing at any one of these disciplines can cause us to descend the ladder, thereby moving us further away from God's will.

Written in Italy during the sixth century, *The Rule of Saint Benedict* was designed to establish the rules by which monks are to live in community. That the *Rule*

31

continues to be observed by Benedictine monks and nuns to this day is a testimony to its many spiritual insights. One of the hallmarks of this work is the idea of a ladder to God. In Saint Benedict's view, this ladder consists of twelve steps of humility. He writes:

> Therefore, brothers, if we wish to reach the highest peak of humility and soon arrive at the heavenly heights we must, by our good deeds, set up a ladder like Jacob's, upon which he saw angels climbing up and down. Without doubt, we should understand that climbing as showing us that we go up by humbling ourselves and down by praising ourselves. The ladder represents our life in the temporal world; the Lord has erected it for those of us possessing humility. We may think of the sides of the ladder as our body and soul, the rungs as the steps of humility and discipline we must climb in our religious vocation.*

It is by humbling ourselves that we get closer to God, and by taking pride in ourselves that we move further away. This medieval twelve-step program often sounds a little harsh to the modern ear. Monks are, for example, encouraged to fear God and to submit almost totally to the will of a superior. Such ideas go against the beliefs that God is love and that blindly submitting to the will

---

* The version of the *Rule* that I am using is *The Rule of Saint Benedict: Translated, With Introduction and Notes* by Anthony C. Meisel and M.L. del Mastro (New York: Image Books, a division of Doubleday), 1975. Used with permission.

of another is as dangerous as it is psychologically unhealthy.

It is easy to discard Saint Benedict's ladder along these
lines. The fact is, however, that the steps of this ladder
contain great truths worth keeping. They only have to
be revised somewhat to account for what we know about
human beings today.

To show this, I offer the following table. On the left-
hand side are paraphrases of what the *Rule* says about
each of the twelve steps of humility. On the right are
modern revisions that I have made:

The Rule of Saint Benedict	**A Modern Version**
1. Obeying all of God's commandments–never ignoring them and fearing God with all of your heart.	1. Obeying all of God's laws with a sense of awe, wonder, and love.
2. Not pleasing yourself but doing the will of God.	2. Not pleasing yourself but doing the will of God.
3. Submitting to a superior in imitation of the Lord.	3. Submitting to a higher cause in imitation of the Lord.
4. In obedience, patiently putting up with everything inflicted upon you.	4. Praising God in all things.
5. Disclosing to the abbot all of your evil thoughts and actions.	5. Disclosing to God (and/ or to a trusted counselor) all of your evil thoughts and actions.

6. Accepting all that is crude and harsh and thinking yourself a poor and worthless workman in your appointed tasks.

6. Accepting life's difficulties and understanding that the world isn't all about you.

7. Not only confessing that you are an inferior and common wretch but also believing it in the depths of your heart.

7. Admitting your imperfections and the need to rely upon God's grace to live with them.

8. Only doing that which is the common rule of the monastery or the example of what your elders demand.

8. Committing to and supporting a God-inspired organization.

9. Practicing silence, only speaking when spoken to.

9. Practicing restraint in speech. Refraining from gossip.

10. Restraining from laughter and frivolity.

10. Not engaging in humor at the expense of others.

11. Speaking gently, without jests, simply, seriously, tersely, rationally, and softly.

11. Speaking gently, without jests, simply, seriously, tersely, rationally, and softly.

12. Showing humility in your heart *and* in appearance and actions.

12. Showing humility in your heart *and* in appearance and actions.

You will notice that a few of the steps have not been revised. This is because these steps can be taken as is. They state truths that are easy enough to understand even from a modern perspective. The rest have been revised to take the edge off of what sounds to the modern ear as too harsh a position. Still, I am hopeful that these revisions capture the essence of what Saint Benedict is saying. Let's take a look at each of these steps in order, considering as we go how we can use these to take on the discipline of humility.

Obeying all of God's laws with a sense of awe, wonder, and love. It is clear by now that humility begins with an understanding of God. Belief implies that there is a God, and also that we ourselves are not God. This brings with it an immediate sense of humility. But you might ask about God's laws. What are these laws? This brings to mind the Ten Commandments, the cornerstone of Judeo-Christian morality. Obeying just these ten is no small feat. Refraining from murder may be easy enough for most of us, but what about refraining from adultery? Adultery is far from uncommon in our society. The same can be said of not worshiping other gods. Many people have made striving for material possessions a kind of god. Even bearing false witness can be difficult. Who doesn't lie a time or two, even if it implicates someone else, just to avoid blame?

The simple act of studying and following God's laws is an important spiritual discipline. It is not enough simply to say that there is a God. We have to see that this God has certain expectations, certain things that we must do and not do if we are to say that we belong to God.

It also helps to obey these laws with a sense of the power that is God. I have read and heard on numerous occasions that fearing God meant something different to medieval writers. For them, fear was closer to awe and wonder. So I don't think it does too much damage to the original text to say that we should obey God's laws with awe, wonder, and love. This puts us in touch with true, God-inspired humility. We see that we are on a path, and that this is a path of great meaning. We sense that God is not distant from us, but very near. In following God's laws, we find a path with heart, one that enables God to increase as we decrease.

Not pleasing yourself but doing the will of God. Again, this is a very difficult spiritual discipline that takes a lifetime to practice and refine. Your strongest instinct is to please yourself and to do your will. Connecting with God and attempting to understand God's will is an extremely important step in the climb of humility. You must spend time with God in order to do this.

Although this is easy enough said, and even easy enough practiced, it is often ignored. I was recently humbled when I spoke to a young woman who had decided to leave work to care for her aging and ailing mother-in-law. She was quitting her job, even though she was well respected and likely to be promoted very soon. Others criticized her about her decision. It didn't seem to fit in a world where people are encouraged to pursue their own goals.

When I asked her how she came to make this choice, she said that she felt it was God's will for her. When I asked how she knew this, she replied that she spent every morning in prayer and Scripture reading, and that she had specifically prayed about this situation. She said that in pursuing this, the response was clear. God wanted her to leave work at this particular point in time to care for her mother-in-law.

I am not arguing that everyone in a similar situation would have to make the same decision as this woman. What I do think is important is the way that she made her decision. She offered it up to God and included it in her worship of God. She sought the will of God, and when she found it, she acted on it. She is an example of humility and discipleship.

Submitting to a higher cause in imitation of the Lord. Here I have changed the wording a bit. You'll notice that I do not say submit to a higher authority, but to a higher cause. Although I think constantly going against those in authority just because they are in authority is counterproductive, I have seen too many instances in which a blind submission to authority leads to problems.

We do know that Jesus submitted to God. We also know that we are to imitate Jesus. Submitting to a higher cause assists us in our imitation of Christ. It requires us to make an extra effort to be of service to others. While we may want to spend our time pursuing our own goals, it is important to ask whether some time may be spent helping the poor and tending to the sick. These are higher causes that Jesus specifically requested that we do.

Praising God in all things. I find "patiently putting up with everything inflicted upon you" simply too harsh for those of us in the world. This might lead the battered wife to stay with her husband, or the otherwise abused not to seek refuge. My reworking of this fourth step in humility is nonetheless difficult. Can the abused wife find a means of praising God in spite of her abuse? I believe that she can, but she must get out of the abusive situation first. All suffering provides us with questions and choices. Are we to be angry all of our lives? Are we continuously to curse God for all of the bad things that happen to us and to those around us?

As I grow as a Christian, I realize how fruitless it is to blame God for the bad things that happen to us. This implies a simplistic view of God. If we please God, some think, life will go well for us. If we don't, then life will go poorly. This approach just doesn't seem to work. Bad things happen to the best of us, and people who should not be abused are hurt. I believe our best hope is to praise God within all of the situations of our lives, no matter how difficult these lives may be. It is here that we find a subtle but powerful force. It is also here that we receive, in love, a lifting of our burdens. But this requires that we, in humility, give up our anger and live in love.

Disclosing to God (and/or to a trusted counselor) all of your evil thoughts and actions. I have heard it said that praying to God is similar to letting the sunlight into a darkened house. In doing this, there are a few rooms that we had just as soon stay dark. These are the rooms that we are either embarrassed about or that we want to keep in their darkened condition. If they were exposed to God's light, we know we'd have to clean them. I am speaking here of our impure desires and our unfortunate habits that we just don't want to release.

Disclosing these rooms to God is an act of humble

submission. As difficult as it may be, there is enormous power here. In submission we realize how frail and human we are. Yet this act opens us to God's love, forgiveness, and strength.

You will note that in this state I have added in parenthesis "and/or to a trusted counselor." The *Rule* has monks disclosing their evil thoughts to the abbot. It is possible for others to follow this method either through "confession" to a priest or a minister. This is an accepted practice in both the Catholic and Protestant traditions. There is also the idea of spiritual direction. Although I have never participated in this practice, I believe that it can be a very powerful experience. Talking over the challenges of your life can be a very powerful experience. As always, you must be cautious to disclose to someone you trust and who is likely to provide good guidance.

Accepting life's difficulties and understanding that the world isn't all about you. Again, I feel that seeing yourself as worthless is too harsh. It simply goes too far and can be seen as indicative of someone with a psychological problem. At the same time, it is important to avoid the equally troubling thoughts and habits associated with narcissism. Narcissists are people who have a hard time understanding that everything isn't about them. They seek to manipulate the world so that it reinforces their own centrality. They become angry and petty when this centrality is threatened.

We all possess a degree of narcissism. We expect life to hand us what we want. I have known people who are in a perpetual state of anger or frustration because they can't find the right job or the right person to spend their life with. These feelings keep them from focusing on how they can be of service to God and to others. The fact is that the world isn't about you or me. It isn't about any of us. Humbly admitting this gives us the freedom to find God where we are.

Admitting your imperfections and the need to rely upon God's grace to live with them. We all have imperfections. Just think of the three virtues that comprise this book. Some have a hard time being humble. Pride gets in the way of whatever situation they face. Others strive for more and more possessions in spite of the fact that this gets in the way of simplicity. Still others feel a need to talk endlessly, regardless of whether or not they really have something to say. In all likelihood, you have a struggle practicing at least one of these virtues.

It helps in humility simply to admit your imperfections and your need to rely upon God's grace to live with them. While such an admission is humbling, it is also enormously liberating. You find yourself giving up the need for perfection and becoming more open to the grace and power of God's love. This is an enormously important step on the ladder of humility.

Committing to and supporting a God-inspired organization. In the beginning of the *Rule,* Saint Benedict discusses the various types of monks. There are monks who stay at an abbey for a time and then move on to another one, just as there are monks who are professional wanderers. Benedict clearly favors those who make a commitment. In fact, stability is one of the primary vows of Benedictine spirituality.

There are two comparisons to make to our experience, both related to humility. One is the need to make some kind of commitment to a spiritually based community. It is simply hard, as well as prideful, to say that you can make it on your own, that you do not need the assistance of any group of people. The fact is that we grow in our understanding as Christians through interacting with others, through being challenged and thinking things through as a community.

The other comparison is our need not just of making a commitment to a community but, as much as possible, making a commitment to one particular community. We, too, can be wanderers, sampling what various churches have to offer. We might feel tempted to stay for a time at a particular church until someone makes us angry or until wanderlust strikes. There are, after all, a number of churches within even small communities. When someone at one church makes you angry, or you have a disagreement of some sort, then the easy thing to do may be simply to pack up and go to another one. Unfortunately, I have found that in leaving one church for another people often confront the same problem as the one that made them leave the previous church.

All of this is not to say that you should never leave a church. Conditions might become so bad, or your beliefs so out of sync, that you feel compelled to do so. But be careful of whim. Humbly think on stability and consider whether you might actually ascend humility's ladder by making a commitment to stay with a church, even when you feel the inclination to leave.

Practicing restraint in speech. Refraining from gossip.
Have you ever worked in or been exposed to a situation
in which there are factions? A friend of mine is currently
working for a company that is going through a merger.
He finds that the merger has created two warring tribes.
Each tribe has different values and different ways of doing
things. Each side feels that their methods and values are
superior. As you might guess, there are a lot of clashes
taking place between the two groups.

Practicing restraint in speech in such a situation is
very difficult. As you will see in later chapters, attending
to your speech is an important spiritual discipline. In a
situation such as the one above, it is very difficult to bite
your tongue and to speak lovingly toward others. Yet
remembering your primary allegiance to God is essential here. Your work is to expand God's kingdom. It is
not to engage in angry words that only make situations
worse.

Not engaging in humor at the expense of others. I must
admit that I would have difficulty restraining from laughter and frivolity as is stated in the *Rule.* Like most people,
I enjoy a good laugh. Moreover, I don't think this is a
bad trait. What is more serious is laughter at the expense
of others. Laughing at the mistakes people make or at
their mannerisms is destructive, even when they are not
present. It harms both the individuals being laughed at
and those who are laughing. There is a subtle sense of a
lack of humility exhibited by the ridiculers. It assumes
that these people have never made a mistake or done something worthy of laughter. Humility calls us to refrain from
such activities and not to participate in pulling people

down through laughing at them, but to build them up through our positive words.

Speaking gently, without jests, simply, seriously, tersely, rationally, and softly. You will notice that this step is taken as it is written in the *Rule*. I felt that it could not be improved upon. There is a very deep truth here. What good does it do to speak loudly, full of jests, and in complex and irrational ways? Yet it is amazing how many people don't follow this advice. Again, pride is a factor. People often feel that due to their knowledge, experience, or some other factor, they can ramble on and on.

I was once impressed in hearing a CEO, a man in his sixties, answer questions from a local news reporter. The occasion was the fiftieth anniversary of the company he managed. He could have gone on and on about his accomplishments and those of the company. Yet his words were the model of brevity and succinctness. When I complimented him later on the speech, I noted to him that it was fairly short. He said that one piece of advice he heeded was given to him a few years ago. The advice was to be especially careful about speaking too long, particularly as he ages. "There is a tendency to want to put in all of your experiences and to ignore the attention span of the audience," he said. There was a strong element of humility in his words. They showed a willingness to focus upon the needs of others as opposed to our own need to be heard and for our accomplishments to be recognized.

Showing humility in your heart and *in appearance and actions.* We have finally reached the last rung of humility.

Again, I leave this statement as is because I believe that it cannot be improved upon. It shows the very deep way in which we are to be humble. There is nothing worse than trying to feign humility. People who do this are easy to spot. True humility involves a deep internal commitment. But it also involves careful attention to our appearance and to our actions. It is not enough simply to think humble thoughts. It is necessary to practice humility in thought, word, and deed. This step is a worthy culmination of all the others. It is the goal to which the practice of humility aspires.

These twelve steps form a solid spiritual practice for anyone interested in taking on humility. It is a difficult task, but well worth it in terms of becoming better at participating in the building of God's kingdom. Climbing the steps allows us to accept our own imperfections and, basically, to get on with life. We become more open to God's grace and acceptance of us. Below is a beautiful statement from the *Rule* that summarizes all of this. Although the passage refers to monks and makes reference only to a male, I believe it can apply to anyone.

When a monk has climbed all twelve steps, he will find that perfect love of God which casts out fear, by means of which everything he had observed anxiously before will now appear simple and natural. He will no longer act out of the fear of Hell, but for the love of Christ, out of good habits and with a pleasure derived of virtue. The Lord, through the Holy Spirit, will show this to His servant, cleansed of sin and vice.

We now have completed a review of the importance of humility. Humility offers great promise, yet it is also a very difficult ladder on which to climb. When I think of my Gethsemane experience in the light of humility, I realize that it has been my pride which prevents me from having more of such experiences. In pride I stop thinking about serving God and spend too much time thinking about what contribution I will make to the world. When I find I am able to ascend the ladder of humility, I experience a great sense of closeness to God. I know something of the joy of my Gethsemane path.

FOUR

The Call to Simplicity

P hyllis had a hard time believing her own words. A tall, slender brunette with a keen intellect and good interpersonal skills, she was doing the unthinkable at her company. She was actually giving up power. For the last two years she had managed three areas of the financial institution where she worked. The two accounting areas were doing quite well, but the third was failing miserably. Phyllis knew that part of the problem was with her. She had been promoted out of one of the high performing areas. She knew how it operated and was able to make it run even better. The second area was closely related to this one, so Phyllis was also able to understand its workings and keep it on track. The third area, however, was unrelated to the other two. It involved legislative relations, a field in which she had little expertise and even less interest.

As a person pegged for rapid advancement within the company, Phyllis knew what she should have done. She should have committed herself to learning about the poorly performing area. But try as she might, she simply couldn't find the time to do this. She took books and articles home in the evening and on weekends, but they sat unread as she spent time with her four-year-old son, Zack, and her husband, John.

Although she felt good about this choice when she was at home, it was always something of a guilty pleasure. Moreover, she could tell that the third area simply wasn't living up to its promise. Phyllis spent her time working with the areas that were doing well and hardly any time at all with the one that wasn't doing so well.

Phyllis made her decision when she saw that reorganization was about to take place. She identified a department where the work of her legislative area was a better fit. The director of this area was more than willing to take on the new responsibilities. Still, sitting in the meeting to make her suggestion, she knew that her decision would likely have lasting implications for her career. Reorganizations are generally considered a time for up-and-comers such as Phyllis to accumulate power. They are ripe opportunities for increasing turf. Yet she was doing just the opposite.

Phyllis was ultimately relieved when her suggestion to move the legislative area was accepted. She no longer has to feel guilty when playing with her son or when she and her husband make a point of leaving work on time so they can get a sitter and go out to dinner. Phyllis and John are working on simplifying their lives even more and have purchased a number of books on the topic. True to her interests, Phyllis focuses primarily on the financial aspects of simplicity. You may be surprised, however, at the source of Phyllis's initial decision to simplify her work life. But more on that later.

Phyllis' decision may be hard for some people to accept. It doesn't fit with a lot of compelling ideas in our society. In many ways we are called not to simplicity, but to complexity. We are told to "be all that we can be" as the Army commercials once said. We should focus on being upwardly mobile, on using all of our talents and abilities so that we can live ever better lifestyles.

The Call to Complexity

One of the most powerful movies I have ever seen on the subject of power and complexity is *Wallstreet*. In this move Michael Douglas plays Gordon Gekko, an extremely powerful businessman who has accumulated money through mastering the art of insider trading. Charlie Sheen plays Bud Fox, a young stockbroker looking to move up in the world. Bud is attracted to Gekko's wealth and power and is eager to form a relationship with him.

There is one particularly telling scene in the movie. In this scene we see Gekko as the model of a man in control of a complex world. In Bud's first face-to-face audience with Gekko, he is invited to Gekko's office and finds him walking on a treadmill and surrounded by a team of assistants. Gekko smokes a cigarette as he exercises. He issues orders not only to those present but also to someone else over the phone. As he is doing this, he is engaging in a conversation with Bud. To me this scene is almost an icon of power and complexity. It shows a man who is seemingly in control of a fast-paced world.

As the movie progresses we see Bud getting pulled further into this world. He finds, however, that this world contains a dark side. The call to complexity is also a call to lose sight of your ethical and spiritual center. Bud ends up not only in trouble with the law, but sadly aware that he has lost a great deal of his self-respect. Of course, we have a number of real-life examples of this, and of the tragic circumstances that often result from a self-centered focus.

Wallstreet shows that complexity can be attractive because it is often closely connected to the accumulation of power. There are other reasons that complexity can be attractive as well. For one, it often seems that this is simply what the world wants of us. We are expected to want to move ahead. We are expected to want to consume more. To resist these expectations is to risk being a loser.

Such expectations have a powerful, yet subtle, influence upon us. If there is anything that keeps people from experiencing what I did at the Abbey of Gethsemane, it is the hectic complexity of modern life. But even in the midst of this complexity we feel the need for a simpler life.

Why the call to simplicity? I believe it can be boiled down to five "senses." These are the senses, or feelings, that we have that appeal to us in spite of our complex lives. The first of these is the sense that the world really has gotten too complex. The fact that you are reading this book now attests to your having this sense as well. It is hard to get away from the feeling that there simply isn't enough time in the day to do all of the things that you are expected to do.

Alex is a friend of mine who told me about his experiences with this feeling of complexity. He was spending almost every weekend either working or taking his children to various sporting events. He decided to take a brief break in between these two activities and go to a local store. This was a "super store" that sold books, music, and computer programs. Alex rushed through the store and picked out a couple of books to read along with three music CDs and two new programs for his computer. He felt a sense of excitement as he stood in line to make his purchases. Then a growing realization came upon him. He looked at the books and tried to remember the last time he had time to read one. Then he looked at the music CDs and had the same realization. He rarely listens to music because of his schedule. Finally, he looked at the computer programs and remembered he already had two programs he'd gotten for Christmas that were still at home in unopened boxes.

It's funny how such a seemingly trivial experience can create a lot of important introspection. Alex put these items back on the shelf and went home to think about his priorities. He asked himself how he could create a little spare time to do such things as read and listen to music. He also committed to spending his money more wisely by making sure that he would really consume what he purchased.

Any number of things might make you feel that your life is too complex. It could be a strong sense of fatigue at the end of the day or a feeling that you are not spending enough time with your family. Depression and feelings of helplessness also result from overly complex lives. As with many things in life, the call to simplicity often begins with the sense that there is a problem.

The next element of the call to simplicity is the sense that it is people that really matter. This is a great truth that we realize from our religion. Jesus focused not on the accumulation of wealth and power, but on the love of others. He spoke of loving your neighbor as yourself and told us that in doing things for the downtrodden of society we were really doing things for him.

The complex life calls us away from such activity. Instead of allowing us to do things for others, this life really blinds us to their needs. I continue to be haunted by a true story that you may have also heard. Seminarians were individually asked to read Jesus' parable of the Good Samaritan and to make a short presentation on it. Along the way to the presentation, which took place in another building, it was arranged that each would run into someone in need. Amazingly, an unusually high number failed to stop and help the person in need. When told that they had to be in a hurry, many literally stepped around the person needing help.

I am haunted by this study because I can see myself behaving in the same way. Among other things, I would not want to risk the shame and embarrassment of being late for class. I would be afraid of being condemned by the class participants and the teacher, as well as fearful of getting behind. If these are general tendencies of humans, as I believe they are, then they are surely multiplied by lives of complexity and haste. The fact is that we are inclined to commit sins of omission and commission when it comes to our treatment of others, and that we need to work along with God to overcome this inclination. Simplicity is a way of finding the grace to do this.

The next sense in the call to simplicity is that of needing to focus more on the planet. This is among the strongest components of the secular simplicity movement. Simplicity means consuming less which, it is argued, is gentler to the Earth. As a result the planet and the human race along with it will enjoy a longer life.

Although many may not claim to be full-blown environmentalists, I am sure that most have concerns about the affects of our lifestyles upon the environment. We have come to accept the *possibility* that burning fossil fuels in large quantities creates changes in the atmosphere that lead to global warning. We do know that certain industrial practices pollute our air and water. We also know that humans have an ever-increasing impact upon the earth's environment.

Consuming less should have a positive impact upon the planet. This makes simplicity compelling, though it points to a seemingly contradictory idea. In attempting to lead the simple life, we are going to have to question a lot of our habits. This at least initially makes life a little harder. For example, simplicity means that we will have to reflect upon the various ways we consume and change our habits accordingly. We may need to take re-usable bags to the grocery store and forego the plastic ones. Or we may have to take the time to take garbage to a recycling center. We will deal with such complicating factors of simplicity in another chapter.

The fourth call of simplicity is the sense that we need to make time for ethical considerations in our lives. As the movie *Wallstreet* so well showed, complexity can lead to immoral and unethical behavior. The more things fill up our lives, the less time we have to consider our actions from an ethical perspective. People often get so caught up in their lives that they tend to lose sight of the ethical dimension altogether.

There are so many instances of this in life that it barely needs explaining. Perhaps the best account of this from my generation is John Dean's *Blind Ambition*, which tells the story of a young lawyer's part in the Watergate scandal. Nowadays we have Enron and Global Crossing as examples of misconduct. Perhaps someone who participated in one of these business scandals will have the courage to write a book about his or her own fall from grace as a result of a concern with leading an upwardly mobile, complex lifestyle.

Simplicity provides more time for reflection upon ethical conduct. If you are concerned with simplifying your life, rather than accumulating power, then you will at least not suffer from the blindness that goes along with seeking status. You may actually stop to help the person in need rather than ignoring that person in the name of honoring a hectic schedule.

The final aspect of the call to simplicity is the sense that we need to make time for God. Spiritual development requires time and effort. Complex lives get in the way of this. Lives often get out of kilter when there is no time for prayer and meditation. This happens when life is filled with social and professional responsibilities. Making a little time for God, whether it is on a daily or weekly basis, makes all of the difference.

Roger is a friend of mine who exemplifies the benefits of such efforts. A research biologist at a mid-size university, he often encounters colleagues who are at the end of their rope emotionally. They are stressed over their status in the scientific community and are concerned about whether they will receive grants to pursue their research.

Roger empathizes with his colleagues. Early in his career he suffered from the same concerns. Just the thought of a proposal presentation would keep him up at nights. On the advice of his wife, he began to attend a weekly worship service. Soon he found that his work was not as troubling to him. He takes a more detached view of his work and makes sure to include time in his week for his family and for a few community efforts. Far from hurting his professional career, he finds that his sense of well-being and peace actually makes him a better researcher. He attributes this to spending an hour with God every week.

Simplicity calls to us as a result of these five senses. These are the senses that our lives are too complex, that we fail to consider others enough, that we are harming the planet, and that we are losing our grip on ethics and spirituality. Simplicity addresses each of these areas. That, I believe, is why simplicity is becoming so popular.

Complicating Factors

Before we move on, however, it is important to think through some of the issues related to simplicity and complexity in our society. This is to keep us from taking an overly simplistic view of simplicity. The fact is that many of the books in this area are a little less than penetrating in their social analysis. If you are really to learn how to live a simpler lifestyle, you have to understand what the trade-offs are as well as the discipline involved. Just telling someone to reduce his or her consumption has the same effect as telling a person to stop eating so much. While we know that reducing caloric intake will result in an obese person losing weight, we also know that it is incredibly difficult for such a person to follow what sounds like simple advice. That is why there is an entire weight-loss industry.

The first factor in a more complete understanding of simplicity is the fact that most of us have to work for a living. We simply can't get up one morning and quit work for the sake of a simpler lifestyle. We have bills to pay and children to educate. And work has several complicating factors. It may require travel or attending social functions in the evenings and on weekends. Moreover, there are a number of informal rules that are asked to be followed. Consider Phyllis' dilemma as mentioned at the beginning of this chapter. As a manager she was expected to want to accumulate more turf. Had she taken this rule seriously she could easily have become overworked in a short amount of time.

The second complicating factor in understanding complexity has to do with the fact that we all share our lives with others. It's hard enough to implement a decision to lead a simpler life. It's almost impossible if those around you do not share your interest. For example, simplicity may require you to spend less time preparing elaborate meals. If your spouse does not share in this, then you are likely to have a lot of friction on a fairly fundamental issue. Without cooperation from the people around you, you are likely to run into a lot of problems as far as leading a simpler life is concerned.

The third complicating factor is the simple truth that

unforeseen events happen to all of us. You may be undergoing an effort to simplify your life when some complicating event takes place. A loved one may become ill or some financial difficulty may confront you. It is hard to change behaviors and habits under such circumstances. So an interest in finding a simpler job, for example, may have to be put on hold while you deal with whatever situation arose. Or the ill health of a family member may make it harder to keep track of your expenses so that you can find ways of reducing them. Your time is spent too much on getting the healthcare needs taken care of for your family member .

By now you are beginning to realize that leading a simpler life is not an easy or simple proposition. Most of us have settled into lives that embody the path of least resistance. So while your life may be complex, it has gotten that way for a reason. It may be because your level of consumption is very high due to some values you hold. Or it may be due to your inability to win others in your family over to a simpler way of life. Finally, it may be the result of unforeseen events with which you have had to contend. Such is the stuff of life.

Pursuing Simplicity

Simplicity requires a lot of critical reflection and effort as a result of the above. We will spend the next two chapters discussing how you can apply such reflection to specific areas of your life. It is important to understand at the outset, however, that you can take steps now to simplify your life. Phyllis is a good example of that. Rather than going along with what was expected of her, she took a conscious step that she knew would make her life much simpler. She also realized that there would be some negative consequences to this step, but she went ahead and did it anyway.

In order to begin the path of simplicity, take a look at some key areas of your life that are creating stress for you. This might be either a work or a relationship situation. Ask yourself what it is about this situation that is creating the stress. Is there some assumption you are holding that you feel you must live up to? Or is there some responsibility you are taking on that you don't need to shoulder alone? Finally, are you talking to yourself in such a way that you are yourself creating the stress?

I'll give you an example of how you can use simplicity to ease the stress in your life. Cheryl is a dedicated parent who has a child that is nearing college age. Extremely concerned with education, Cheryl experienced a lot of anxiety over where her daughter, Jamie, would go to school. Cheryl wanted the best for Jamie, who is a bright girl with an outgoing personality. Cheryl knew that the state university was the cheapest, but that it was considered to be an average college. There were several private colleges nearby, but they were considerably more expensive. Jamie would need to get a scholarship in order to attend one of these universities. Like many sixteen-year-olds, however, Jamie lacked the motivation and organizational skills to pursue the number of scholarships she would need to obtain to go to one of these universities. A single parent with a demanding job, Cheryl simply didn't have the time and energy to help Jamie very much with scholarship applications. Cheryl's constant nagging of Jamie to find and complete scholarship applications was becoming a sore point in their lives. It threatened to ruin the final two years of Jamie's time at home.

Admitting defeat, Cheryl contacted the state college and found out that they have a scholars program for particularly bright students. These students attend high quality, challenging classes. Many of them have gone on to receive full scholarships to go to graduate school. All of this for the same price of a public college tuition. Cheryl realized that although Jamie seemed to lack ambition now, she would probably grow out of that and by the time she was in college. As a result, Cheryl decided to enter Jamie into the scholars program. She didn't need to complicate her life with taking an additional job or even spending the time and effort it takes to apply for multiple scholarships. She also didn't have to make Jamie's life difficult by putting a lot of pressure on her to be "scholarship caliber" as a high-school junior.

This is an example of how you can use a little reflection to simplify your life. It is a matter of looking at your assumptions and seeing if you can accomplish goals without expending more time and effort than you have to give. Simplicity demands that we lead a more reflective life and make choices according to this life. Although it does include some work at the beginning, there is a payoff in the end as far as not spending beyond your means, both in spending money and in spending another precious commodity. That commodity is time.

Simplicity calls us to ease the complexities with which we have filled our lives. Do we really have to run in circles trying to take care of so many things at the same time? Can we get by with less? Can we take the time for considered reflection upon our lives? These are important questions.

Perhaps the most important question of all concerns whether you are making enough time for God. I believe that this in and of itself is a powerful simplifying force in life. Recalling Phyllis' situation, remember that I mentioned there was one particular influence in her decision to reduce her responsibility. A daily Bible reader, she came across Romans 12:2 in which Paul advises us not to be conformed to this world. This made her realize that in attempting to continue to manage the legislative area she was conforming too much to the world of her work. She was getting away from what she knew to be more important. She wasn't serving God. Although some may disagree with her decision, it simplified her life and allowed her to spend more time with God and her family.

The rejuvenating aspects of simplicity make it an important discipline to undertake. Simplicity allows us to spend more time with God and to experience the great joy of that experience. More than that, it allows us to bring the fruits of this experience into daily life. Like humility, it provides endless opportunities for living life with God.

FIVE

Practical Simplicity

Early twentieth-century British writer Evelyn Underhill once wrote a book entitled *Practical Mysticism*. The title of the book is as perplexing today as it was many years ago. We tend to think of mysticism as being anything but practical. Practicality is more in the realm of daily life. When we tell people to be practical we are asking them to give up wild notions that simply won't work in reality. Ideas and thoughts associated with mysticism are often thought of as being among these wild notions.

Yet mysticism, for all of its vague and ethereal connotations, is helpful to having a life of meaning. When I think of mysticism, I think of being connected to God. Without this connection, life seems harsh and cold. With a daily, practical connection to God, I am able not only to withstand the difficulties of life but can also reach out to others and connect to them. If mysticism is to be meaningful, it must have this practical bent.

Simplifying life connects quite directly to the idea of having a spiritual or mystical connection to God. When we allow life to drain us of all of our energy, then it's hard to reach out to God. It is equally hard to be open to the experience of God in daily living. We lose the sense of practical mysticism. God becomes a distant concept, something that we ignore or even think skeptically about.

Practical mysticism requires practical simplicity. You have to find ways of simplifying your life in order to experience the love God. In this chapter we will look at ways to make simplicity practical and will create a simplicity plan. We will also discuss specific tools you can use to create this plan. This is an important project since there is an overabundance of information on simplicity. If you are to practice this discipline, you need to break it down into components that you can use.

Listed in italics below are three assignments for you to perform as part of simplifying your life. All the supplies you need for these are a pen or pencil and some paper. You'll want to review the tools listed in the rest of the chapter before completing the third assignment. These will help you create a plan that is both practical and specific to you.

Your first assignment is to conduct an honest assessment of the complexities of your life. This requires you to do the following:

Write down on a sheet of paper all of the compli-cating factors in your life. This can be any item, ongoing event, or person in any area of your life. List not only the things that seem to steal time, but also the issues that rob you of your energy. Be sure to leave enough space between the items to do some additional writing. You will be doing that in the next step.

Most of us can list our energy drainers without a great deal of thought. It might be that you have to go to a lot of meetings, or that you have to spend a lot of time doing busywork. It could also be a boss or coworker who makes a lot of demands of your time and taxes your emotional energy. Please take the time to list these now.

Now it's time for the next step in this process. Why is it that you experience the items on your list as troubling or complicating? This question underscores the truth that life is comprised not only of what is presented to us but also of how we react to what is presented to us. What may be complicating or troubling to you may not be to someone else. Do the following to get a more complete picture of this:

Consider each item on your first list individually. Write down next to each item what it is that makes this item complicated or worrisome to you.

You are going to need to do an honest self-assessment here. Think, for example, about having to deal with a difficult person. If you have a coworker who causes you a great deal of heartburn, don't just get caught up thinking about this person's negative traits. Consider what it is about this person that makes *you* react negatively to him or her.

As you complete this assignment, think of what you know about yourself. Are you an introvert or an extrovert? Are you a controlling person, or do you like to leave the details to someone else? What kinds of people bother or irritate you? What are some of your positive and negative characteristics?

In answering these questions, it helps to remember the things that people have said about you in the past. Contained therein may be some clues about why certain people or events bother you. Also recall personality profiles that you may have taken. Many of these offer helpful clues to your reactions.

Armed with a list of complicating factors in your life, as well as ideas about why you experience these factors as complicating, you can now move on to the next step. Here you will work with the two previous assignments to come up with a means of dealing with the complications that bother you. Take these two assignments and, along with the tools you'll be given in the balance of this chapter, do the following:

Create a plan for reducing the complicated and stress-producing factors in your life. This plan should identify the more complicated areas of your life and include specific steps or tools for addressing these. Be sure to include deadlines as part of your plan.

An important feature of this plan is that it will be designed specifically for you. You have identified the complicating areas of your life and why you find them difficult or complicated. The plan you develop will take into consideration not only the things that are particularly stressful or complicating for you but will also include steps that take your unique reactions to life's events into consideration.

To create your plan, rank the items on your original list of complicating factors. You will be working with the top three factors. Take a sheet of paper and write your most complicating or stressful factor on it. Use the results of the second assignment to come up with a complete statement of why this factor is particularly complicating or troublesome. Next, create a list of steps you can take to make this factor less complicating. Finally, put deadlines to each step and list some dates for you to check your progress.

Go through the same process with the next two highly rated complicating factors in your life. After you do this, take a look at all three of the factors as a whole. Ask yourself if you can perform each of the steps for each one. Make adjustments where necessary and then put your plans for each one in final form. Finally, take a cover sheet of paper and write a paragraph describing in general what you will do to reduce complexity with respect to these top three factors and set dates for reviewing your progress. Weekly progress checks are usually a good idea. Put this cover sheet with the other three in a folder that you can readily access throughout the week.

Once you are satisfied with your progress on the most highly rated items, consider whether you need to move on to create a plan for the next three complicating factors. If your life still seems too complicated, then it is a good idea to move on to these. If you are satisfied with the level of simplicity in your life, then you can stop the process at this point. Put your work in a place where you can review it in the future. If you ever begin to feel your life is becoming complicated again, repeat this process exactly as above.

At the end of this chapter, we'll take a look at an example of how applying this approach can help ease a complicating situation. For now let's consider some tools that you can use in filling out the steps of your plan. These tools may be used singly or in combination to attack any problem. This is not meant to be an exhaustive list. I'm sure that with a little effort you can think of some others. These do provide a good start to dealing with many of the complicating features of life.

Delegate or share tasks. This classic tool in effective management may be used by anyone who is facing a complicating situation. New managers typically become overwhelmed by their desire to handle all problems themselves. Many fail to make the shift from doing things themselves to getting things done through other people.

The same is true of many people when faced with a difficult situation. It may be that you have had to assume the care of a loved one who is in ill health or that you have had some other complicating factor come into your life. Your first inclination is to shoulder the burden alone. Remember, however, that it doesn't do much good for you to become burnt out as a result of taking on more than you can handle. Ask yourself who or what can help you deal with the situation.

Understand your limitations. Behind delegation is an important realization. No one person can do it all. This tool is a clear recognition of that. Be realistic about what *you* can do. I emphasized you in the previous sentence because each of us has unique strengths and limitations.

Being realistic about yourself allows you to make plans to deal with your limitations and to draw on your strengths and compensate for your weaknesses. Andrew is a friend of mine who manages a group of computer specialists. Chief among his strengths is the ability to foresee problems and to make plans to overcome them. A weakness he has is his tendency to avoid face-to-face confrontations. To overcome this weakness he has someone on his staff whose judgment he trusts to tell him when he is avoiding a problem he should be handling. He has promoted this person to deal with the more minor problems while he still deals with the major ones. This frees up his time to do the problem solving he excels at while also making sure that he is involved with the major issues that could disrupt his area.

It is important to understand that neither this tool nor the previous one should be used to avoid responsibilities. It creates a lot of ill will for someone to take all of their tasks and push them off onto other people. As with anything, a certain amount of discretion and common sense must be displayed in using this tool. Still, understanding your limitations and delegating or sharing tasks are invaluable in dealing with the complicating factors that you face.

Prioritize. One of the staples of personal planning is the need to prioritize. We face so many tasks in our daily lives that it is difficult to do them all. By prioritizing tasks we are better able to do the ones that are important to us.

There are several time-management programs that emphasize prioritization. I would encourage you to look into these and select the one that you feel would work best for you. Most plans ask you to divide your tasks into three or four categories. The top category consists of tasks that you absolutely have to do quickly. The next category includes tasks that you need to at some point, but not today. The lower categories are items that either have a long time line or simply aren't that important to accomplish anytime soon.

I maintain a list of activities that I need to complete and go through a prioritization scheme each day. I select those things that I am going to do today and assign them a high priority. I may go back to the list if it appears that I will have more time that I originally thought. In my "A" list I not only include items I feel pressed to complete or make progress on that day, but also items that are interesting to me or fit with my life plan. This makes my day more enjoyable and ensures that I will work on things that are valuable to me.

There is one additional approach I use to my list that is somewhat at odds with the conventional wisdom on prioritization. I allow time each week to complete the lower priority items on my list. If I didn't do this, then these items tend to stay around without getting done. Typically these items aren't particularly difficult to do and have some importance to me as an individual. For whatever reason, I find gratification from taking a little time each week to get these done and cross them off of my list.

Prioritization is enormously important in simplifying your life. This tool is part of a general approach to making sure that you spend your time doing activities that you have to get done. It can also be used to ensure that you take the time to perform tasks that are important to you. A priority list can also serve as a barometer of how complicated your life is becoming. A large list full of high-priority items means that your life is getting too complex. When you see that happening, take a moment to reassess your situation and make some changes.

Manage information. A modern complicating factor of life is the ever-increasing amount of information that we have available to us. We are flooded with information from television, newspapers and magazines, and the Internet. Along with the information is the fear that if we don't read or listen to it all, then we are likely to miss something terribly important.

E-mail only complicates this situation further. People in business often receive numerous e-mails while on the job, and can receive still more on personal e-mail accounts at home. Many also belong to "listservs," which are e-mail distribution lists designed to keep people informed of late-breaking news in a particular area.

This large amount of information undoubtedly contributes to the feeling of information overload. How to deal with this situation? I recommend a three-step approach to help you to handle the information overload you may be experiencing.

The first step is to find the best news summary that covers your area of interest. This could be either print or electronic. You can use this as a bulletin to alert you of important news in your area of interest. You can also drill down into key areas of interest. More importantly, you can replace many of your existing sources with this one source. This may include magazines, listservs, or other items that may be cluttering your physical and electronic mailboxes.

Following the first step, the next step is to take a look at all of the magazines and other materials you receive. Ask yourself if you are willing to budget time each week to read these services. If not, get rid of them. Cancel the subscription or unsubscribe to the listserv. This will not only save you time and money but also get rid of that nagging feeling you have when you haven't read every item that comes your way.

The third step is to set aside formal time each day to answer e-mails and read your important information. It is easy to become consumed by answering e-mails as they come in. At the end of the day, however, you may find that that is all you have accomplished.

The opposite is often true of the important documents and other reading material that you receive. We often set these aside and don't spend the time necessary reading them. Or, we may put these off until we get home and then either get side-tracked by an activity or lack the mental power to read the documents carefully. Set aside some time each day to read what you consider to be important. I've found that setting aside about an hour to read e-mails and thirty minutes for other reading material is adequate for both of these activities.

Organize. Good organization is another effective means of simplifying your life. This includes organizing your work area effectively. Create a filing system that works for you so that you can easily store and retrieve items.

This also includes organizing files on your computer so that you know where important documents and e-mails are.

As with prioritization and time management, there are many good books on organization. The main aspect of organization is that it takes an investment of time to establish an effective method. Ironically, you'll have to invest some time now in order to save it later. This is time well spent, however. Think of all of the time you have spent in the past trying to retrieve something that you just couldn't find.

Think creatively. Complex situations often involve problems that need to be solved. As such, it helps to apply techniques from creative problem solving to arrive at new and innovative solutions. There are several books on creative problem solving, and I encourage you to look into this topic to see what will work for you. One technique that I have used with success is to pick a word at random from the dictionary and apply it to whatever complicating situation I may be facing. The word will likely have nothing to do with the situation you are facing (if it does, pick another one), but it will force you to look at the situation in a new light.

A similar tool from creative problem solving is to take an idea from a totally unrelated field and apply it to the situation. If you are an engineer, for example, and are spending a lot of time dealing with an engineering problem, try thinking of the problem from the perspective of medicine. This, again, provides a new look at the issue.

A final creativity technique is that of discussing the problem with someone totally removed from the situation.

There are two advantages to doing this. For one, it makes you boil the issues down into simple, understandable terms so that someone outside the situation can understand it. This in itself can cause you to question your assumptions and come up with new solutions. It also opens your mind to the opinions of someone that may have fewer biases and will certainly take a different perspective on the situation.

Pray. Prayer is always a good idea. You can use prayer in many different ways when dealing with complexity. For one, you can make a direct petition to God to help you deal with the situation and to find ways to simplify it. I find it helps simply to discuss with God the situation and then clear your mind to see if anything comes to mind. Additionally, look for ways throughout the day that God will be responding to your prayer. Remember that God always takes the long view, so you may not get exactly the type of response that you think is appropriate. You will, however, be able to benefit from God's grace with respect to the situation if you simply open your heart to him and expect results.

Apply the Scriptures. Another way of seeking God's guidance is to think meditatively upon Scriptures. Take your favorite Bible passage or verse, for example, and read it slowly. Allow it to seep into the fibers of your being. Then think about the situation you are facing. Hold the thought meditatively in your mind and then open your mind to simplifying ideas that come from this.

Another simplifying practice is to read passages from the Bible as part of your daily routine. Set aside time each day to do this. Read the passage and hold it in your mind. Then consider what this passage is saying to you. How can you alter your life to fit what the passage means? Many times you will find a simplifying message in such an exercise.

Adopt healthy habits. These are the types of habits we read or hear about in the news every week if not every day. By healthy habits I mean eating healthily, exercising, and getting enough rest. It is amazing how complicated life feels when we fail to do any one of these things. In order to eat healthily, reduce the amount of fat in your diet and stay away from candy and other junk foods. To exercise, set aside time each day to engage in some kind of physical activity. Proper rest involves getting enough sleep each night. It's true that complexity and stress will get in the way of each one of these activities. People who are stressed tend to eat more, less healthy foods. They also have a harder time exercising and are frequently up at night worrying about some situation that they must face.

When you are facing such a situation, remember to come back to the basics of a healthy lifestyle. It is amazing how much better life looks after a good night's sleep. It is also amazing how much better you will feel after you begin eating a healthy diet and exercising. Ever-growing evidence supports this, but you have to do more than listen to the evidence. You have to act on it.

Let go of ideas or practices that create stress. Many complicating factors of life are self-made. Anyone with teenagers knows that at some point they start pursuing goals

that interest them rather than those that interest you. I
once thought of my son becoming a great baseball player.
During the early part of his life, he had the same vision.
When he reached adolescence, however, baseball was no
longer interesting to him. I tried hard to keep him interested, but soon realized that I was creating a lot of stress
for both of us. I was creating a complex situation. Once
I let go of the idea that my son had to be a great baseball
player, the situation dissipated and both of us were happier.

You now have tools to create a plan for dealing with
the complicating factors of your life. I will give you a
brief example of how some of these tools can be used
before turning this exercise over to you. Let's say that
one of the complicating factors of your life has to do
with a chronic lack of money. You are constantly short
of money and are considering taking another job to make
ends meet. You know that this would take valuable time
away from your family, however. You really aren't sure
how to deal with this situation, but know that it creates
a lot of stress.

Applying the above tools can help you in numerous
ways. Letting go of ideas and practices that create stress
would be the place I would begin. It may be that you are
spending money unnecessarily on things that you really
don't need. This is a common problem in affluent societ-
ies. Prioritizing can also help. This will enable you to
consider what activities and goals are really important.
You may be spending money to achieve goals that are
not a high priority.

Prayer and Scripture reading are also important. Here
you will find guidance as far as dealing with the situation

in a healthy and holy way. Again, you may find that your money worries are self-imposed. Should you in fact need to take a second job, you are going to have to do some thoughtful delegating. This tool will enable you to avoid the trap of trying to do it all when you have to take on additional responsibilities. Remembering to practice healthy habits is a tool that will help you to keep your life in balance as you consider both the situation and what you have to do to address it.

By now you see that simplifying your life is a conscience activity. It involves thinking through issues and considering how you can make your life less stressful. If anything, simplicity is a great adventure. If you can let go of our society's push to complexity, you will discover that there are a number of ways that you can lead a less stressful life. The best means I know of is to sit down and think through exactly how and why your life is so complicated, and then create a plan to do something about it.

All of the above may seem a little out of place for a book coming from the realm of spirituality. It is important, however, to put some feet on your spirituality from time to time. It is one thing to read and think about the benefits of a simpler life, and quite another actually to do something about it. Simplicity is a discipline, and like any discipline, it requires a little work and self-sacrifice to do well. The benefits, however, are great.

SIX

—

Simple Riches

C onsumer reduction, environmentalism, and personal finance are among the most widely
addressed aspects of simplicity in modern times.
These three ideas are often linked in the popular literature. The argument is that reducing the consumption of
goods creates less waste and is, therefore, gentler to the
planet. Reducing consumption requires conscious effort
in the area of personal spending. The added benefit to
this effort is that if we decrease our consumption, then
we can also decrease the amount of time we work. People
might even get to the point where they are financially
independent and able to live off of their investments.

Published in the early 1980s, Duane Elgin's *Voluntary Simplicity* is in many ways the foundational work
of contemporary thinking about simplicity. It embodies
the environmentalist "less consumption" view expressed
above. Another extremely important book focusing more
on personal finance is *Your Money or Your Life* by Joe
Dominguez and Vicki Robbins. This popular book features a rigorous program for attaining financial independence through a reduction in personal spending and

conservative investing. This program is associated with the less consumption/environmentalist viewpoint.

In many ways the current interest in simplicity can be attributed to these two works. Both capture interests that have been going strong for a number of decades. Environmentalism is an almost unconscious concern for many people today. It is among those small group of concerns that managed to survive the 1960s and 1970s. At a minimum, we all want to live in a world with clean air and water.

Many also desire to achieve financial independence. As the baby boom generation ages, there is a growing interest in leaving often well paying but stultifying jobs. Many dream of being able to tell the boss good-bye and going out to engage in more meaningful activities.

I will focus my comments here on personal finance because this is the engine that fuels much in the area of consumer reduction, personal growth, and environmentalism. But more important than this, at least for our purposes, is that personal financial management is a major component of a simpler life. It means not consuming so much, which in turn means not having to spend so much time working to pay the bills. This leads to a simpler life.

Your Money or Your Life is perhaps the leading book on personal financial management in the simplicity movement. This is a place it well deserves. The book features a rigorous program to put a person on the path to financial independence. Among the steps involved are finding out exactly how much money you have earned over the course of your lifetime and taking stock of all of your assets and liabilities. You are also asked to determine how much of your time you actually spend working (which includes commuting time and time spent worrying about work). This figure is divided into your wages to so that you can determine your true hourly wage. You are then encouraged to think about how many hours you actually had to work to be able to afford whatever item you are interested in buying. The book also asks readers to keep account of every penny they spend and to create an investment plan so that they can plot exactly when earnings from their (conservative) investments will allow them to quit their jobs (or at least gain the freedom to find more satisfying work). Not surprisingly, Dominguez and Robbins frown upon such activities as shopping.

The popularity of *Your Money or Your Life* is well deserved because I believe that those who are able to follow its steps to conclusion will indeed have put themselves on the path to financial independence. The downside is that it takes a Herculean effort to complete all of the steps, and the authors as well as adherents of the book insist that all of the steps must be followed as closely as possible. I myself have read the book twice and attempted to put the program into practice in as many times, only to fall short on both occasions.

There is, I think, a twofold problem with the book. For one, it requires a great deal of self-discipline to complete all nine of the steps. The step of coming up with an exact figure of how much money you have earned over the course of your lifetime is difficult, as is taking a complete stock of your assets and liabilities. But these efforts pale in comparison to keeping an account of each and every one of your expenses. I found keeping up with everything from the quarters I put into parking meters to the coffee I buy at the coffee shop in the morning to be a daunting task. In the end, I simply gave up.

A second part of the problem is that the Dominguez and Robbins program requires a high degree of cooperation among couples and families. This is often unrealistic. I may be a big believer in the program, but that doesn't necessarily mean my wife and children are as well. Unless they are willing to keep an account of every penny they spend, then my efforts will be hopelessly incomplete. Moreover, my efforts to win them over to the program may end up causing a great deal of friction. I have painfully discovered that discouraging my wife and daughter from shopping not only creates a great deal of hostility toward me, but it also robs them of some precious time that they can spend together in doing something they both enjoy. While Dominguez and Robbins may frown on me about this, the frowns I have received from my family are much worse.

For me the *Your Money or Your Life* program is simply impracticable. Does that mean I am hopelessly lost as far as simplicity is concerned? I remember several years ago a book was published entitled *The Lazy Man's Guide to Enlightenment*. The book was written for people who wanted to be enlightened, but didn't want to engage in the rigorous practices that many religious programs require achieving this end. In that spirit I offer some ideas for people like me who find the ideas from Dominguez's and Robbins' book too difficult to implement. These steps may serve as a short-term program until your situation changes so that you can begin something that is more complete. In any event, please accept these five measures as a sort of lazy person's guide to personal financial management and simplicity.

The first step to take is to find ways to use your computer to save time and to arrive at a better understanding of your finances. This means purchasing a money management program. If nothing else, such programs make reconciling your bank statement at the end of each month a relatively painless process. These programs offer several other timesaving and eye-opening advantages. For one, you will be able to tell very quickly where most of your money is being spent in any given period of time. If you enter the information fully and accurately, customized reports will provide you with your earning and spending categories. This will give you a better idea of where your money is coming from and where it is going. You may be able to use this to make some quick adjustments to your spending habits and to increase the amount of money you save. You can even use such computer programs to establish a budget. Advanced users can delve into still further applications, such as establishing and monitoring a college savings plan or creating a debt reduction program.

There are other ways you can use your computer to simplify your finances and to save time. Many banks feature on-line bill payment, for example. This enables you to pay bills without having to go through the trouble of addressing and stamping envelopes and putting your payments in the mail. You can also authorize some monthly bill payments, such as utilities, to come directly out of your account. Some may feel a little hesitant about allowing even a utility to have access to your account. These same people may also be leery of on-line bill payment for fear that this also exposes their bank accounts to security risks. If you are one of these people, then don't use these approaches. The main point is to find ways to make technology work for you. When I was growing up, technology was touted to be the great simplifier of life. In many respects it isn't. If anything, life has become more complex as a result of technology. Who could have predicted ten years ago, for example, that many professionals would end up spending huge amounts of time responding to e-mail. With a little thought and effort, however, some technologies can be used to live up to the dream of simplifying life.

The second step to take in a lazy approach to financial planning is to determine your savings goals. What are your short-term and long-term goals? Take out some paper and actually list your goals in each area. Among your short-term goals might be getting out of credit card debt, having a will drawn up, taking a trip, saving enough for Christmas, or giving a certain amount of money to charity. Your long-term goals might be educating your children, saving enough for retirement, or paying off your mortgage.

You may wonder why this is the second step in the process instead of the first. The first step of using the computer is helpful in a couple of ways. Getting a software program to help you track your finances is often a dose of reality. It helps you to see how much money you spend and where you spend it. This should give you a realistic perspective when you start setting financial goals. You may want to retire by the time you are forty, for example, but your computer program may make you realize that you can't do that when you spend so much money dining out. You immediately know that you are going to need to make some trade-offs. The second realization that arises from analyzing your computer data is that you must fund your goals. This is the third step in our process.

Funding your goals means that you set aside enough money to be able to achieve them. Start with your list of short-term goals. How much would you have to spend to achieve each one? Some of these will be quite easy to determine, while others may take some time. You may know, for example, how much money you plan on spending for Christmas or how much you'd like to contribute to your church or to charity. You may not know how much it costs to have a will prepared. Look into those issues where you have questions and get a figure and write it down on your list. Remember, too, that you will also need to budget time as well as money for some of your items. If you want to have a will created, for example, you'll need to schedule some time to do this.

Next, take a look at your long-term goals. Again, figuring out how much you need to fund these goals is going to be easy in some areas and hard in others. If you want to payoff your mortgage, for example, the amount is easy enough to determine. Saving for a college education is something else entirely. It depends on where you would like to send your child or your children to school and how much the cost will be when they are ready. Still, there is fairly good information on such issues on the Internet, for example. Another difficult area is that of saving for retirement. It's difficult to predict what the cost of living will be in several years, as well as how much money and assistance will be available in such programs as Medicare and Social Security. Moreover, as we have recently witnessed, it's hard to determine where and how to save for such long-term goals. Putting all of your money in the stock market can result in substantial losses, as well as substantial gains. How do you plan to meet goals given this amount of volatility?

There is no easy answer to this last question. I tend to side with the *Your Money or Your Life* authors in sticking to conservative investments that are not prone to fluctuations. In so doing you can better predict what your return will be and how long it will take to save to achieve your goal. I realize, however, that this goes against much of the conventional wisdom of investing. This wisdom tends to favor taking on some degree of risk in order to enjoy a return higher than the inflation rate. There may be no lazy approach here. If you are interested in taking on some risk but potentially maximizing your return, then learn more about this subject or perhaps seek the services of a financial planner whom you can trust. As far as figuring out how much your long-term goals will cost, do give that a little time and come up with a figure that you feel is reasonably accurate.

After you go through this exercise with both your short-term and long-term goals, you should now have some idea of how much each of your goals costs. Now sit down and determine how you can fund these goals. If you want to pay off your credit card debt within six months, figure out how much you will need to pay on the card for the next six months. Do the same if you want to take a trip in the next year. Do the same for your longer-term goals. Finally, devise a plan to fund both the long-term and short-term goals and put it into action. It may mean contributing a certain amount to your 401K every pay period, for example, or setting up a savings account and putting enough money in each month to pay for your Christmas and trip-planning expenses. It could also involve sitting up an educational IRA for your children and contributing to it on a monthly or quarterly basis.

I do want to mention one approach that is even lazier but still provides some measure of savings for your goals. It may be, for example, that you really can't find the energy to determine how much money it's going to take for you to retire. The variables are just too great and your spare time too small. What you can do instead is to figure out how much money you feel comfortable putting aside for retirement. Some financial planners encourage a minimum of 10 or 15 percent of your income for retirement. In any event, while you may not arrive at an exact date for your retirement in doing this, you will at any rate be saving something. The same approach can be taken with respect to saving for college education. Rather than figuring up an amount to the penny and saving for it, ask how much you feel comfortable putting aside, and do that, realizing that while it may not be enough, it will at least provide some amount of money.

I'd like to mention one short-term financial goal you should have before proceeding to the next steps. Many financial programs mention the need to have a certain amount of money set aside for emergencies. You need to have money set aside, for example, in case you lose your job. Most programs recommend having enough to cover a minimum of six months of living expenses, or six month's salary. It is hard to refute this wisdom in today's economic environment. One of your first goals should be to set aside enough money to cover at least six months of living expenses should you lose your job. This money should be conservatively invested and easy to get to. Be sure you fund this goal early in your savings program.

The next step in the lazy person's guide to financial management is to live as modestly as you can off of what you have left after savings. By taking the above steps, you have in essence removed a certain amount of money from your income. The result is that you have less money to spend then would otherwise be the case. Using your money management computer program, you can keep a running tally of how much money you have left. When your account gets low, you know it's time to stop spending.

This approach forces you to spend less without forcing you to adhere to a budgetary amount in all areas of your spending. You now have a plan that creates savings for your goals while also letting you live your life without having to continue to worry about exactly where all of your money is going.

I do, however, have a couple of cautions regarding this approach. For one, it is important that you not save so much for your financial goals that you can't live on what is left. You will likely need to adjust the amount of money you set aside for your various goals. Another issue is that you don't allow this plan to get you into credit card debt. Don't use your credit card to make up for shortfalls as you save for your long-term plan. You will only be robbing Peter to pay Paul, as the expression goes. Finally, expect unanticipated financial issues to arise. John Lennon once said that life is what happens while you are making other plans. I have found that hardly a month goes by without some unexpected expense coming about. You may have to purchase a new set of tires for your car, or your mortgage company may inform you that you are not putting enough in your escrow account, or you may have an unexpected medical cost. Such is the stuff of life. Try as best you can, however, to continue to fund your financial goals while living off of the rest. Remember, too, to review your goals periodically, making adjustments as your income changes or as your goals themselves change.

One final area of financial growth has to do with growing your areas of enjoyment at work. This is somewhat at odds with the program outlined in *Your Money or Your Life*. There the idea is to save enough money so that you can go off and pursue your dreams. For the reasons I mention above, I think that this approach is simply impracticable for most of us. It's too hard for most of us to save enough money to start looking for "meaningful" work within a reasonable amount of time. The alternative I offer is to find areas of your current job that you can enjoy and see if you can expand them so that you get more of a sense of satisfaction out of your life. This idea is consistent with ideas found within Martin E. P. Seligman's book, *Authentic Happiness*. I encourage anyone interested in happiness to read this book. Seligman is a psychologist who has spent his life looking at such traits as optimism and happiness. His latest research suggests that people are happiest when they are performing activities that they are good at and that they enjoy.

The more you are able to do that, the more you will be able to experience happiness in your current work. I mention this as a goal related to personal finance because for many leaving their current job would mean losing something in terms of pay and benefits. Growing where you are planted is a good way of achieving financial stability while meeting your financial goals.

From a purely spiritual perspective, there is likely to be a lot of good you can do at your work. Many people feel that they must quit their jobs and join the Peace Corps in order to do some good in the world. This often simply isn't the case. Many businesses have a strong commitment to the community and are happy to support their employees in spending at least some of their time in a worthwhile humanitarian effort. There is also a lot you can do in your regular work to extend the kingdom of God. Simply listening to the problems of a coworker or helping someone at work you know is having a rough time is an important effort you make. Giving a portion of the money you make to a deserving charity is another way of helping others. Finally, doing the best you can at your job has merit, particularly when you offer these efforts to God. The old Shaker expression, "Hands to work and hearts to God," has a way of transforming both yourself and the workplace when put into practice.

The simple financial plan outlined above may leave something to be desired in terms of being particularly inspirational or earth-shattering. Funding your goals and living within your means is not something to ignite religious or spiritual fervor. Moreover, much of what I have said above is distilled from various other works on personal finances. There is so much sound advice out there that it is difficult to come up with anything particularly new.

There is a great deal to be said, however, for taking a simple program such as the one outlined above and putting it into practice. It provides a certain peace of mind as far as knowing that at least your major goals are identified and that you are doing something to reach them. The more automatic you can make your plan, the easier your financial life will become.

There are two other issues that need to be mentioned before moving on to our final topic of silence. The first is how humility and financial planning actually complement each other as far as creating wealth is concerned. Thomas Stanley's and William Danko's *The Millionaire Next Door* shows how people with a humble mind-set, that is those who don't feel they have to buy a lot in order to appear well-to-do, actually have a greater chance of accumulating wealth. In other words, there is something to the idea of simple riches. Stanley and Danko found that many people in highly compensated occupations don't have much in the way of savings. They spend too much of their money on fancy cars and big houses. Those who have managed to save a lot of money are often the people next door that no one notices because they don't lead a lavish lifestyle. They are busy saving instead of busy spending.

This brings us to our next point. While it is certainly a good thing to save, you also have to be careful not to become so attached to your money that it becomes the ultimate focus of your life. It is all well and good to lead a frugal life and, as I argued above, to put yourself on a plan to meet your goals. Yet know that life holds inevitable surprises for us. So while you save for your goals, you must also hold onto your possessions very lightly.

You never know what the world, or what God, has in store for you. You don't want to be like the rich young man and fail to follow Jesus into building the kingdom of God because you are so attached to your wealth, even if you did work hard to earn it.

As I reflect upon my Gethsemane experience I realize that worry about money is one of the main reasons why I miss those moments of pure lightness. Financial worries often keep me from enjoying God. When I can come to balance my financial responsibilities with my desire to enjoy God, then I am going a long ways toward finding this experience once again. But that also requires that I move from simplicity to the topic of silence.

SEVEN

The Beauty of Silence

We live in a noisy world. The streets are noisy, offices are noisy, and meetings are noisy. As we drive home we are likely to reject silence in favor of the radio or music of some sort. When we arrive home the television may well be going full blast. Even when we lie down to sleep, our heads may be filled with noise. Many people have trouble getting to sleep because they are replaying conversations they have had, or would like to have had, during the day. Some also wake up in the middle of the night with worrisome words going through their minds. A quiet mind is a rare thing to have.

Confronting the world with silence can be a difficult prospect. For one, we have gotten used to the noise. It is uncomfortable when it isn't there. That's why many people immediately and unconsciously turn on the television when they arrive home. I have one friend who attended a retreat at a facility that didn't have any televisions in the guest rooms. He found himself looking for the remote as he plopped down on his bed at the end of the first day. He continued to do this even after the second day.

Another issue is that noise expects noise in response. We often feel as if we need to be heard in order to justify our presence in the world. The person who doesn't talk is often seen as someone who isn't contributing. That's one reason why meetings are filled with people droning on and on about something that could be said in a brief amount of time. Such people are asserting themselves, making their presence known.

As we saw in chapter 3, three of the last four steps in Saint Benedict's ladder of humility deal with speech. These are practicing silence, restraining from laughter and frivolity, and speaking gently and without jests. Those of us living in the world can also practice these steps by listening to how we speak. Do we talk so much that we emphasize our own importance over that of God and others? Do we engage in humor to the extent that we aren't serious enough about life? Do we make fun of other people, damaging reputations for the sake of a laugh?

Although there are places in the Bible that indicate silence before God (Habakkuk 2:20), silence is not necessarily a virtue that we are explicitly encouraged to practice at all times. Yet paying attention to our speech is important if we are to act ethically and spiritually. Such guidance as doing unto others as you would have done unto you certainly involves speech. You would not want people talking badly about you or making fun of you. Jesus condemned the Pharisees for the way that they prayed out loud, putting their piety on display for the world to see. The implication is that spirituality has a quiet, private element to it. Jesus telling us not to worry about tomorrow in the Sermon on the Mount also has a speech element to it. Worry, as we will see, involves the kind of things you say to yourself. To follow Jesus' words means not to be consumed with worrisome thoughts.

The beauty of selective silence is that it deepens us spiritually in so many ways. By selective silence I mean both picking specific times to be silent before God as well as practicing restraint in speech throughout the day. We will explore these aspects of selective silence in this and the following two chapters. In this chapter we will look at silence before God, specifically as it pertains to prayer. In the next chapter we will look at silence, or restraint in speech, in our social relations. The chapter after that will look at silence in relation to the self. These chapters together provide some general ideas on how to undertake the discipline of silence in a world as noisy as our own.

Prayerful Silence

Prayer is a difficult topic on which to write because there are so many practices and diverse schools of thought. One practice is to use prayer as a means of simply talking to God. This approach is well examined in a book written several years ago by Barry and Ann Belford Ulanov called *Primary Speech*. The idea is to bring your thoughts and troubles to God and engage in a conversation with God about them, seeking guidance, wisdom, and understanding. The Jesus Prayer, found within the spiritual classic, *The Way of the Pilgrim*, takes a different tact.

Here we are to pray a set prayer at all times. This prayer is "Lord Jesus, Son of the living God, have mercy upon me, a sinner."

Centering prayer is a practice that is growing in popularity. With roots that go back to the medieval book, *The Cloud of Unknowing*, this practice encourages people to select a word that means something to them spiritually and meditate upon this word for twenty minutes in the morning and in the evening. Yet another popular practice encourages a routine in prayer. The acronym "ACTS" is used to describe one such practice. This prayer begins by the one praying *adoring* God, then moving to *contrition* in recognizing our sins and asking for forgiveness. The one praying should next offer *thanksgiving* and praise to God, and conclude with *supplication,* or requests, for God's help on matters that are troubling.

This, of course, only scratches the surface when it comes to prayer. There is also the Lord's Prayer given to us by Jesus, as well as the Prayer of Faith which healers such as Agnes Sanford use. The prayer of Jabez, recently popularized by a bestselling book of the same name, comes from a passage in the Old Testament. This prayer is intended to bring peace and prosperity to those who pray it while serving the Lord. *Lectio Divina* is yet another type of prayer or meditative practice that has Christian monastic roots. This involves taking a small section of Scripture, reading it aloud slowly, and prayerfully considering both its historical and personal meaning.

With so many different practices in existence, it is hard to choose the one that is best for you. Some prayer counselors encourage people to look into their own personalities to find the type of prayer that works best for them. "Pray as you can, not as you can't," as one member of the clergy once told me.

How does all of this relate to silence? Obviously some types of prayer are more geared to silence than others. Centering prayer, for example, is likely to lead to moments of silence when the word one is using fades and there are times when nothing is being thought or said. This contrasts with those types of prayer that involve either a set routine (ACTS) or discussions with God (Primary Speech) which are less likely to bring about interior silence.

What I would like to argue is that silence is an important part of whatever type of prayer you may use. It can be as much a part of prayers, such as ACTS and Primary Speech, as it is a part of Centering Prayer and the Jesus Prayer. Adding moments of pure silence can enhance many of these practices. At some point, after all, we need to be quiet. There are three distinct benefits that silence adds to our prayerful practice. Let's take a look at each of these.

The first benefit is that of finding guidance. This relates particularly well to those types of prayer that involve asking for God's help with respect to a particular problem. By incorporating silence into your prayer you open yourself to the possibility that God will actually respond to you. Many times we get so focused upon our worries that we can't stop talking. This only aggravates whatever problems we may be having. We "grow" our problems to the extent that they become insurmountable. To put it indelicately, at some point we just need to shut-up and listen to God.

An interesting part about the practice of silence in prayer in this way is that it teaches us to be silent and watchful outside of prayer. It is my experience that when I take a specific problem to God, and then am silent about it at some point after the prayer, I may not get a particular answer during the silence. Yet through a kind of "watchful waiting" that my silence has taught me to use throughout the day, some answer will come to me during the course of my ordinary activities. In other words, through practicing the same type of silence in my daily life as I practice during prayer, I am more open to the various blessings, graces, and messages that God has for me. Often this involves specific guidance with respect to the issues I have prayed about.

The second benefit of adding silence to prayer is that it allows you, if even just for a brief moment, to lose yourself. Part of the problem of being a human being is that it is hard not to be self-centered. This brings along with it such things as worrying about our reputations in the present, replaying the bad things that have happened to us in the past, and worrying about the future. These activities all lead to unhealthy living.

Silence in prayer allows you to forget about yourself for a while. You can experience that blessed moment where you dissolve and fade into pure contemplation and being before God. The idea of dying to yourself is a strong one within the Christian tradition. How better to die to yourself than to experience this death in prayer and to carry something of this death over into your personal life. We hear in the Prayer attributed to Saint Francis that in dying to the self we are born again. How better to die to the self and be born again then to practice silence? In silence you stop the internal dialogue that keeps you alive to yourself.

The third benefit of silence in prayer is that it creates the experience of God's love. This is often a related experience to dying to the self. In dying to yourself, you are freer to experience the joy that is God. Many people are simply too busy to experience this love. They are so caught up in their lives that they can't pause long enough to know God. This may even be true in their prayer lives. People spend so much time thinking about their problems that they don't open themselves to the joy of God. Silence can fix this.

Another problem is that some people feel that they don't deserve God's love. This may be due to things they have or haven't done in the past. Silence can be an antidote to this problem. By suspending your thoughts you can open yourself to the love of God. You can even begin the experience of healing from something. Silence creates an emptiness that allows space for God's healing love. Most of us, unfortunately, have the feeling that we have come up short on something. We've disappointed someone, hurt someone, or simply done something that we should not have done. Silence opens you up to the love of God. Silence creates the space through which God heals.

By now I hope that I have convinced you of the important of silence in prayer. The next question is how to incorporate this into your daily practice of prayer. To begin with, it is important to note that most people don't use any one practice to the exclusion of all others. Many draw from several different practices, using one or two throughout the day. I have also found that there are times when I will favor one particular practice and then switch to another in order to keep my prayer life fresh and alive.

I have, for example, changed from contemplative approaches to more conversational types and then back again, according to what I felt best fit me at the time.

Silence has a place in whatever your particular practice may be at a specific point in time. It always helps to clear the mind and be silent before God—no matter what type of prayer you may be praying. If you already practice a contemplative type of prayer, such as centering prayer, than silence is probably a part of your prayer life anyway. There are likely to be moments when the word that you are using fades away and you experience pure silence. As for other types of prayer, you can simply incorporate a period of silence after you conclude your prayer. You can empty your mind, concentrating on nothing. I find that it helps to empty your mind with the purpose of filing it with God. In other words, empty yourself and just let yourself be before God.

The easiest way to do this is simply to plan for a moment or two of silence after your prayer. Quiet your mind and think of nothing. If you find yourself thinking about some issue or trying to solve some problem, simply let it go. Return back to the silence. After a period of silence, allow God's love to become a part of you. Feel God's love entering into your mind and reaching into your heart. Feel it in your very bones. Feel this love changing you and healing you. Open all of yourself to this love, even the parts of yourself that you are ashamed of or don't want God to know about. Then gradually come back to your wakeful state and return to your activities.

After Prayer

Incorporating silence into your prayer life easily spills over into silence in your active life. I have a practice of saying brief prayers during the day, followed with a moment of silence. This allows me to cope with whatever stressful moment that I may be facing. It's as if the prayer quiets the mind, and then the silence further clears it. This helps me to remember that whatever difficulty I am facing will pass, just as my earthly life will pass. I can better realize that I don't need to be overly worried about what happens.

Another aspect of silence before God is to plan a period of extended silence. This can be anywhere from a half day to a weekend or even an activity that lasts all week. Many retreat centers offer programs that are in fact extended periods of silence. Some focus upon a specific theme, such as healing, while others invite participants simply to be silent for several hours. Benedictine retreats are another activity that allows you to enjoy periods of silence. In these retreats, participants live the life of a Benedictine nun or monk through incorporating periods of prayer, praise, and silence. Such retreats can last a weekend or a week.

There are more informal types of silent retreats you can take. Many monasteries will allow people to stay in guesthouses so that they may use this time as a period of reflection. You just need to make arrangements beforehand with the abbot.

Even less formal is simply picking a spot to get away from it all and using that as a period of rest, reflection, and silence. A friend of mine has a practice of once a year selecting areas that have particular significance to her. Over the past few years she has visited places of historical significance, as well as the restorations of various Shaker communities. Each time she comes back with new insights into her purpose in life.

I believe that most people have locations that are important to them and that can serve as powerful centers for prayer and reflection. Often we put off visiting these, thinking that we'll get to them at some point in our lives. Life is all too short, however, and it is important to occasionally answer the call to spiritual growth that such areas are making. Set aside a weekend, or even just a day, to venture to such a spot and quietly think about what this journey is saying to you.

Taking a retreat of any type that incorporates silence can be an important means of finding and experiencing God. It is important to know a little bit about yourself before taking such a retreat. There are times when it is good to take such a retreat, just as there are times when it is not so good. If you are experiencing a time of difficulty or trouble, for example, then a silent retreat may be the last thing that you need. Some people may end up using such a time to ruminate upon their problems, causing the problems to grow even larger. It would be better for such people to find an activity to occupy their minds rather than trying to empty their minds. Conversely, some people may need a period of reflection during times of difficulty.

The best means of understanding when a good time for you to go on a retreat is simply to look at how you have handled difficult situations in the past. If you have returned from such retreats better equipped to deal with the situation, then that is a good time for you to go on a retreat. If instead you found that it was best to get away when you were relatively trouble free, then you should look for those instances to incorporate an extended period of silence in your life.

The fact is that people are different and you need to be attuned to what your dispositions are. This not only helps in determining how to handle an extended period of silence but also in how to handle brief periods. If you have a hard time being alone, then prayer, particularly contemplative prayer, may be hard for you to practice. If you are more introverted then you may be drawn to contemplative prayer and to extended periods of silence. It may be more difficult for you, however, to put into practice insights gained during your times of silence, or to see God in the various situations of your life that involve people, because such instances tend to sap you of your strength.

The key is to balance the ways you are comfortable with prayer with the ones that are a little uncomfortable. An extrovert who practices contemplation and silence may have a hard time of it, but such a person is likely to gain something by going through the experience. Similarly, an introvert gains by seeking out situations with people and looking for ways to practice the fruit of his or her contemplation. It certainly is not the case that you should seek out the opposite of whatever you are naturally inclined to do. That involves too much of a denial of the self. What I encourage you to do is occasionally to incorporate the opposite into your life. Realize that this will be an effort, but also realize that it will provide you with some impetus for spiritual growth. In any event, everyone benefits from some type of silence in their lives, whether it is a brief moment or a more extended one.

One other aspect of silence before God that I would like to explore is that of grace. Grace doesn't really follow a pattern or respond to a formula. It is always there for us to experience. Often we simply ignore this experience. The Gospel according to Luke tells us that the kingdom of heaven is within us. I believe that this means that the experience of God and God's grace is always there for us, we just have a hard time seeing it.

Silence before God opens our eyes to this. My simple prayer in the shed at the Abbey of Gethsemane opened my heart and mind to God's grace. It opened me to that different world where the prayers of the future could be experienced in the present and where lightness can be felt even in a time of difficulty.

I believe that Jesus' advice in the Sermon on the Mount is also applicable to these thoughts on silence. Jesus tells us not to worry about the future because worry doesn't add anything to our lives. Interestingly, he does not tell us that we can be totally free from worry. He simply says that the worries of today take up enough time.

It's hard to exaggerate how helpful this advice can be in your life. If you are one of the many people who have a tendency to worry, then the future can seem like a frightening place. Following Jesus' advice, you need to learn to let go of these events and concentrate on what is before you. Jesus does not say that we should be unconcerned about what is immediately before us. If we did that, then we would never take any action to protect our families or ourselves. Clearly, there are times when such action is necessary. Yet we can develop an attitude where we can handle the situations before us without worrying excessively about the future. After all, as Jesus said so well, all of our worry will not add days to our lives or keep us from dying earthly deaths.

Silence before God has a way of reminding us of this. It keeps us open to the fact that we must face what we must face, but we should do so with God's help, grace, and knowledge. This has a way of making the future fears we have vanish and opening us the grace that keeps us focused on the present.

We live in a noisy world. There is a constant sense of motion and of sound. The noise can be overpowering sometimes. To overcome it, find the space for silence in your life. Incorporate this silence in ways that are comfortable, and occasionally in ways that are uncomfortable. Use this time to feel the love of God. Take this love with you and experience this love, through silence, throughout the day. And be ready for the joy this love brings. In a world as busy as our own, we need this.

EIGHT

The Way of Restraint

Kyle was angry with his son, Nathan, as they drove to his friend's house. Nathan and his friend Joe were working together on a homework assignment for school that was due the next day. Kyle was angry because they had put the assignment off until the last minute. They could have easily completed it over the weekend. Had they done so, Kyle wouldn't have to get out after a particularly trying day at work. As they drove along, Kyle couldn't help but lecture Nathan about the need to get tasks done earlier. Finally, after Kyle had been talking nonstop for five minutes, Nathan decided he could take it no longer.

"The trouble with you is that you see everything as a problem. You've wanted to meet Joe's dad anyway, so why don't you take this as a chance to do that."

Nathan's words struck home. His sixteen-year-old had really pegged him on this one. Kyle does tend to see everything as a problem, and he did want to meet Joe's dad.

Joe's father is in the music business and Kyle wanted to talk to him about his experiences. They ended up having a very nice evening. Kyle enjoyed a fascinating conversation while Nathan and Joe completed their assignment.

Kyle learned something about himself from his son that day, but it required a degree of restraint and humility to do so. He learned that there is a great deal he can learn from his son if he would only be quiet and listen. He also came to the realization that he can be overbearing sometimes, and that this robs not only his happiness but those around him as well.

All parents should understand the importance of speech in their relationships with their children. I know that like Kyle there are times when I go too far with my children. Both from fatigue and from a desire to teach some lesson that I feel my children need to learn, I can easily launch into lectures that serve more to alienate than to instruct. Of course there are times when my children need to learn lessons. Still, it does little good constantly to hound them about some point. I need to be judicious in my speech, practicing restraint and seasoning my words with understanding.

Restraint in speech, or selective silence, is an important part of establishing harmonious relations with others and of leading a generally peaceful life. We have already seen how important this idea is to Saint Benedict's ladder of humility. Restraint in speech is found in his admonitions to practice silence, to avoid laugher, and to speak gently and without jests. You may remember in chapter 3 that I changed two of these steps so that they reflect a healthier practice. These became refraining from gossip and not engaging in humor at the expense of others. I left speaking gently and without jests alone because I feel that this way of putting it cannot be improved upon. The idea behind all of these is that attending to your speech is important to your soul life. Not practicing restraint in speech damages us in some way. We fill the world with empty words and leave a sense of our self-importance. We also make it harder to silence our internal dialogue. If you are forever wondering what you will say next and what someone else will say to you in return, then your mind is filled with endless chatter.

Honoring the silence means practicing restraint in speech. This is as important at home as it is at work and other social settings. We have already seen an example of how too much talking can create problems at home. Dealing with children is joyful, but can also be difficult. Older children in particular begin to challenge the rules that parents make and the words that they say.

Parents need to reflect upon what they say to their children, as well as on how often they say it. Many people nowadays want to make sure that their children are able to excel and secure good jobs in the future. As noble as this is, it also creates a lot of stress upon children. Sometimes it's good simply to learn to put restraints upon such topics.

I will return to Kyle and Nathan to make this point. Kyle is concerned with where Nathan will eventually go to college. In the past he has hounded Nathan about preparing for the SAT and doing the kind of activities that he will need to in order to get into a top level school. He has also pressured Kyle to think about where he wants to go to school and what he wants to do.

As a typical sixteen-year-old, such thoughts are far

from Nathan's mind. He really doesn't know what he wants to do with his life, and would rather do any number of things than spend extra time preparing for a test. Kyle's past lectures to him on such topics have only served to make him somewhat depressed and cranky.

Luckily, Kyle began to realize that he was doing more harm than good. He began to practice an extreme form of selective silence when it came to such topics with his son. He realized that once he started talking about the subject of the future with his son that he became negative and really wasn't communicating effectively. He also realized he was ruining what could well be the last two years that his son spends at home. Kyle decided to squelch his desire to talk about the topic and began to trust his son to find the future that suited him. As hard as this was, practicing this type of selective silence resulted in much better relations between the two of them.

Selective silence can improve marital relations as well. Many couples experience difficulty with particular topics. These typically involve such issues as child rearing, money, and relationships with extended family members. Of course it is important to come to some kind of general agreement on such topics. Yet once these agreements are reached it is often best to speak sparingly of them. Continuing to focus on trouble spots often just makes situations worse.

Incorporating silence into your relationship with your loved ones pays large spiritual dividends, both for you and your family. Speech is always a double-edged sword. What you say to your family influences the quality of their lives. This, in turn, affects yours. When Kyle practices restraint in speaking with his son he finds that he feels much better about himself. He lets go of his need to create a perfect child and discovers the joy of a better relationship with his son. This also causes Kyle to feel better himself.

Again, it is important to strike a balance here. There will be times when you need to say something in order to prevent someone you love from making a mistake. There are also times when you need to talk about something that is important to you. You don't need to keep your feelings to yourself on such occasions. What I do encourage you to do is to focus on areas in your relationships at home where your words may be doing more harm than good. As an experiment, try talking minimally about such issues. See if refraining from speaking about them helps the situation improve, or at least creates more harmony in the family.

Restraint in speech also helps situations in the workplace. In your work life you have probably encountered a lot of situations in which it would have been better for the people involved to practice some restraint. People seem naturally to gravitate to conflict and to think the worst about one another. These tendencies play out in work situations every day.

The rapidly changing face of work these days only compounds these tendencies, Mergers, acquisitions, and corporate restructurings create a lot of tensions. Such situations often have the unintended consequence of pitting one area against another. As the areas come together to form a business relationship, people on one side may feel superior to people on the other. People on the other side may feel suspicious and threatened by the part of the company that is merging with them. The situation worsens as people start to look for the worst in the op-posing group. Negative comments and gossip becomes rampant. The result is an environment that is hardly conducive to spiritual growth.

Even without constant restructuring, the workplace can be a place where a lot of negative speech takes place. To combat this, try some of the following steps to see if you can put into practice more spiritually guided speech habits at work.

One habit to adopt is to only speak the truth. This one simple principle can have an enormous impact in your relations with others. Keep idle speculations to yourself so that they don't take on a life of their own. If someone passes along some information about another person which is not totally verifiable, then refrain from passing that along to someone else. More positively, in meetings limit your speech to stating in a few words what you feel is a particularly true observation. I know of one execu-tive who has used this to good advantage in his career. He is not the person who talks the most at meetings. In fact, he tends to be one of the quieter ones. But when he does speak, people listen because they know that he has something important to say. His few words usually belie great insight. As a result he is well respected and seen as a straight shooter who knows the business and doesn't baffle people with confusing statements.

There is one literary example of this kind of approach. Ernest Hemingway is known for his straightforward prose. His short stories are models of brevity and insight. He once said that in his short stories he tried to express one truth. He wasn't trying to capture a range of truths, nor was he just stringing together random observations.

He was expressing one idea that in his experience he found to be true. If you adopt the same approach in your communications, you will become an effective communicator. You will be putting selective silence to good use.

Another practice you can adopt in your speech is not to engage in gossip. There is so much gossip that goes around these days that it's hard not to become engrossed in it. We seem to be a very judgmental people, and don't need much to get our judgment going. Not engaging in gossip means not passing along negative pieces of information about others that are of a questionable nature. Again, a little common sense has to be exercised here. For example, you would want someone to tell you if there were a rumor that the person you were about to get involved with in a business deal had swindled other people in the past. Unless there is some compelling reason to do so, however, it is best not to engage in idle talk about what others may or may not be doing. I have found that, more often than not, gossip about other people simply ends up being untrue.

Restraint in speech may also be practiced by not mocking or making humorous comments at the expense of others. People often make careless or cutting comments about people who are different from them. These may be people from a different ethnic background, or perhaps people who were simply brought up to be different than they were. Restraint in speech means simply not focusing negatively on people's differences, even if it will get you a laugh in a meeting or in a conversation.

But what about the foolish things that people so often do? It is hard not to focus on these and either to make fun of them or get angry about them. Restraint in speech means paying attention to your reactions and stopping before you speak or act. It helps to remember some of the foolish things that you have done. I am often puzzled in driving when I see someone get excessively angry about a minor incident. Perhaps someone is trying to get into another lane and nearly hits another car because that car is in their blind spot. The driver of that car becomes extremely angry and starts gesturing and screaming. Sometimes such a person will even pull out a gun and start shooting. Of course you know that such individuals have committed their own driving mistakes in the past. We all have. You wonder why such people cannot be more forgiving of others.

Another element of restrictive speech has to do with restrictive listening. You need to attend not only to what you say, but also what you listen to. All people are influenced by what they hear, and we do have some control over this. Listening to "adult oriented" material with a lot of profanity will make it seem okay for us to use this type of language. Seeking out people who use this kind of language will also influence the way we talk. Can we do something about this? To use another example from American literature, I've heard that William Faulkner would never listen to an off-color joke. He happened to be someone who enjoyed hunting and would go on hunting trips in the backwoods of Mississippi. Hunters like to tell jokes and stories, of course, and when Faulkner could tell that the story was getting to be of a crude nature he would walk off a ways from the group until it was over. Now it's probably not the case that we would all feel comfortable doing such a thing. What we can do, however, is to find ways to limit our listening so that we don't learn bad habits from others. In work situations we can learn to limit contact with those who have only negative comments to make or who are always looking for the worst in people.

The last element of restrictive speech that I would like to mention is that of refraining from making comments that others will see as pointless or frivolous. This is difficult because often there are issues that you feel are important to you and should, therefore, be important to others. You have to be careful not to drone on and on about such issues in meetings and in private conversations with others. To get at this, it helps to take a page from public speaking. In public speaking courses, you are encouraged to understand the needs and interests of your audience. To hold the audience's attention, you should speak to those needs and interests rather than speaking to your own. This keeps the audience's attention and keeps you from boring them with your issues.

You can effectively speak in a meeting, and practice restraint in speech, by understanding your audience. Think first about where they are coming from, what issues they have, and what constraints and interests they have before speaking. This will help you to get your points across more effectively and to be less likely to bore your audience.

This brings up the issue of when you should speak. We have talked so much about restraint in speech that we really need to address when it is important or necessary to speak. As always, the lives of Jesus and his disciples are good examples here. Jesus spoke not to establish his self-importance. If anything, he was very humble in his speech. If anyone had justification for making grand claims about himself, it was Jesus. He spoke with modesty and refrained from advertising his status, really looking to others to form their own conclusions. Yet he did speak with authority when it came to interpreting the Scriptures and when it was a matter of rebuking those who were going against the will of God. He backed up those words with actions, as we see in the case of the moneychangers in the Temple.

We see the same attitude in the disciples of Jesus. Paul and others refrained from speaking frivolously and out of self-importance. Yet speak they did, realizing that this was the best way of spreading the Gospel. They were also quick to speak against those who got in the way of this effort.

What does this say to people living in modern times? Jesus put it best when he said let your yes be yes and your no be no. In other words, don't fill the world with all kinds of frivolous statements. Say what you mean and say it simply.

As to the content, it helps to focus on a few key factors when you speak. I summarize this by encouraging you to speak truthfully, speak wisely, speak lovingly, and speak sparingly. Speak truthfully by saying only what you know to be the truth. Don't speak lies or half truths. In our society it is often common for people not to tell the truth. This is often because we don't want to be held responsible for whatever our actions have created. We can get around this by telling some kind of half truth. We see people doing this on television all of the time. In fact, it is a common plot on many programs for one of the characters to feel that a lie must be told in order to keep something bad from happening. As a result I think that we all have less of an aversion to lying than we should. Speaking truthfully, however, is a standard measure of whether you are exercising virtue in your speech. Look at your own speech to see if you are in the habit of not being totally honest when you talk to others. If you aren't, work against this.

Speaking wisely means to speak with all of the knowledge that you have about a particular situation. On the positive side, recognize that wisdom comes from God. Some people are too shy to speak, and often don't let their thoughts and opinions about a particular situation be known. Many tragedies could have been averted if someone had just had the courage to speak what they felt would be the wise thing to do about a particular situation. Honor the wisdom that you possess, and speak it when it will do some good. Conversely, refrain from speaking authoritatively about issues on which you have no special knowledge or guidance. It's okay to say that you don't know much about a particular topic. There is nothing worse than someone acting like they have all of the answers about everything. If you don't have anything wise to say about a particular topic, consider not saying anything at all.

Speaking lovingly is the most important part of the statement above. Make sure that your statements are made with the well-being of others in mind. This approach will keep all manner of sins from creeping into your words. It will keep you from gossiping when you know such gossip damages yourself and others. It will help you to speak supportively to those who are in need of support. It will also teach you to pause before you speak so that you prayerfully determine whether it is best to speak or to be silent in a given situation. Your concern will be how your words can have the best and most loving impact.

Speaking sparingly is a topic that we have already addressed throughout this chapter. This means simply to say less and to listen more. Weigh the impact of your words before speaking or writing them. Don't feel that you have to say a lot in order to be heard. Concentrate instead on speaking what is truthful, wise, and loving.

It's important to understand that it is not always possible to satisfy truth, wisdom, love, and brevity in your speech. Anyone who has taken an ethics course knows that there are situations that arise where it is impossible to speak both truthfully and lovingly. The most famous examples involve those where telling the truth will harm someone in some way. If someone wanted to kill another person and the would-be killer came up and asked you where a gun was, and you happened to know where one was, are you obligated to tell that person the truth?

Unfortunately, we live in an imperfect world where situations such as this can arise. Again, love is your best guide here. Determine what response is the most loving one, and make that response. This will be the one that protects the well-being of others or furthers God's kingdom in some way. Realize, though, that ethical dilemmas are exceptions and not the rule. They should not be used as an excuse for constant lying. That sort of behavior often ends up hurting others in incalculable ways.

Speech is so important to the way that we interact with the world. Think about this the next time you are involved in a difficult or stressful situation. Think about how much speech is a part of the situation. It may be that the lack of speech is creating a problem, or it may that too much speech is creating a lot of pain.

Recently I heard something Mahatma Gandhi said that put much of this into perspective. He said we should be the change that we would like to see in the world. In other words, instead of lamenting the fact that there isn't enough love in the world or that the world is imperfect in some way, we should act according to the way that we would like to see the world. Such an attitude, as Gandhi's life shows, can have an enormous impact.

In facing a difficult or stressful situation, you would obviously like the world to be a different way. This way might be more loving, or more forgiving, or something else along those lines. If you can start to embody that change, then you are taking great positive actions in your life and in the lives of those around you. Often these actions for change come in the form of speech. Speaking truthfully, wisely, lovingly, and sparingly about a particular situation can make a difference. It brings you closer to God's kingdom.

Many of us face situations such as Kyle faced with Nathan at the beginning of this chapter. We get into habits where we fail to listen and learn. We speak excessively out of fatigue, habit, and a general belief that we are right. Kyle learned a great deal about communicating with his son, and with others, by listening to what his son had to say. He learned a great deal from Nathan's heartfelt observation. We are all likely to learn much from those around us if, in humility, we would simply listen to what they have to say. In order to do this, it helps to practice restraint in speech, or what I have called selec-

tive silence. This silence can create lasting change in our
lives and can open us to the joy that God can bring to
our relationships with others.

NINE

The Silent Self

I'm going to tell you something that a lot of the self-help literature, particularly that which is spiritually based, tends to ignore. This is that worry and stress are an inevitable part of life. So while you may think you can free yourself from fear, there is likely something that will come along to make you afraid anyway. Trying to be silent in all things will not totally rid you from stress and worry. Even joining a monastery won't do this. Nuns and monks also suffer from anxiety, anger, and other day-to-day annoyances.

I think that Jesus' words in his Sermon on the Mount affirm this. He tells us not to worry so much because doing so won't add any time to our lives. He also tells us not to worry about what we will eat and how we will cloth ourselves. We should not even worry a great deal about the future. But he adds to this the statement that today's worries are enough. So although we should limit our worries to what is before us, there will be situations that arise that we must deal with today. The key is to let God work in our lives so that these concerns are manageable. They become concerns that we focus on at particular times of our day. We don't allow them to consume our lives and our focus. We put these worries in their place.

Perhaps a good distinction here is between worry and fear. Worry is something that in a limited way is good. A little bit of worry keeps us from acting dangerously or haphazardly. If I had no capacity to worry at all, then I might start coming to work whenever I wanted to, unafraid of losing my job. I might even stop worrying about turning off the burner on the stove, no longer afraid that the house could burn down.

Problems start when such "helpful" worries become fears. If I worry so much about keeping my job that I become absorbed by it, then I am acting out of fear. If I am so worried about my house burning down that I can't leave it without checking the burner a hundred times, then I am acting out of fear there as well.

Fighting Fear

We know from the Scriptures that perfect love casts out fear. A good antidote to all consuming fear is to focus on the love of God. This reminds us that God loves us. No matter what happens to us, we have the assurance of victory in the end. Given the normal stresses of life, however, it is by no means easy to get to the point where we are no longer afraid and our worries are limited along the lines of Jesus' advice in the Sermon on the Mount. People today have to worry about such things as losing their jobs due to economic downturns and the break-up of their families due to divorce. Added to this are new and growing concerns in such areas as terrorism and identity theft. These are not abstract threats. I have known people who were headed toward the World Trade Center when the planes crashed into it on September 11. Had they arrived fifteen minutes earlier they would have been victims. Not one, but three people in my immediate environment have had to deal with the theft of a credit card number in the last year. Divorce and job losses are also impacting people that I know. Such things could happen to any of us.

There is a lot to worry about, and there is a lot to be fearful of. Although it is impossible to get rid of all the worry in your life, there are ways to reduce it to manageable levels. One of the best ways is to practice silence. This means focusing upon the constant chatter in your head and decreasing the chatter that creates stress and anxiety. There are three major ways that you can introduce silence into your life in such a way as to help deal with fear.

The first way has to do with practicing silence itself. This means introducing periods of silence throughout the day. I have already discussed how you can add silence to your prayer life. In order to become proficient at creating silence, it is helpful to set aside specific periods of the day both to pray and to be silent. Sitting aside some time in the morning, however brief, to commune with God and be silent with him is a good way to start out the day. It sets the tone for the day and makes a great deal of difference as far as facing the day-to-day challenges that we all face.

It also helps to set aside some time at midday to pray and be silent. I grant that for many of us this will be a difficult task. People working in cubes and offices may feel a little self-conscious about praying in their work areas. This can be overcome by silently reading a brief piece of inspirational literature and inviting the silence into the rest of your workday. Again, I have found that doing this at midday helps me to face the challenges of the afternoon when I am often fatigued but still must face issues and problems. It is also helpful to clear out a little time at the end of the day to pray and to be silent. This can be achieved by snatching fifteen or twenty minutes either before or after dinner. This pause helps you to deal more effectively with family issues. These can be just as difficult as the work issues you face during the day. It helps to deal with these after a period of silence. Finally, it is enormously beneficial to create a little silence just before you go to bed. I have found that being silent and spending some time with Jesus helps to put away problems that otherwise might haunt me in the night.

The second major way you can deal with fear is through taking the time to deal with the problem. Take whatever it is that is bothering you and spend some time thinking about what you should do about it. Create a plan to address it. Give yourself as much time as you need to do this, though I have found that most plans only take a few minutes. Write down what the problem is and think about what you should do about it. Give it your best effort. Once you do that, think about when you will do it. Plan whatever needs to be done in the next few days to address the problem. Then plan to take another look at it after a few days have passed.

After you have created your plan, simply forget about the problem. You now know what you have to do. You have given the issue your best attention and you have planned accordingly. It often does little good, and actually some harm, to continue to think about a problem and spend your time second-guessing your decisions. You will be addressing the problem when you perform whatever activities or take whatever action you have planned. Give your mind a rest from it during the times when you aren't doing these activities.

Forgetting about the problem is often difficult. This brings us to the third major way you can deal with a fear or a problem. It helps to practice another form of selective silence with respect to fears. That is, to be silent about the particular issue that is troubling to you and to focus your mind on something else. This helps you to compartmentalize the problem. There are several ways of doing this. One is to find some distraction so that your mind stays busy thinking about something else. Work is always a good distraction. Focusing on a project or a task helps to distract you. You can often get some useful work done as you do this.

Another activity is to do something like watch television or listen to the radio. Such passive activities often get bad press in religious circles. Yet I find that at the end of the day it is enormously relaxing to find some program that is uplifting or moderately educational. Granted there is a lot on television that isn't worth watching. Those programs that are sexual or violent in nature aren't really helpful as far as cultivating silence. Yet some programs can offer some much needed distraction and relaxation without the sex and violence.

A third activity you can undertake is to exercise. Exercise is a great way to distract your mind and to cope better with situations. Moreover, exercise provides a bodily release from anxiety and has been proven to elevate good cholesterol and lower blood pressure. You can also practice silence as you exercise. You can put your mind on automatic pilot when you do an activity such as running. Just make sure that you don't become so oblivious to your surroundings that you put yourself in danger!

Practically any activity that you enjoy is a good way of taking your mind off of problems. I know from experience, however, that it can be hard to make yourself to do other things while you are preoccupied with worry. Some events simply strike us in a very visceral or bodily way. The heart starts pounding and the stomach turns independent of anything we may say or do. We automatically slip into a "flight or fight" response which no amount of silence or distraction can prevent.

I have found the following method helpful in dealing with such instances. To begin with, it helps to recognize that you are traumatized at the particular time that you first become exposed to the concern. Particularly if you are someone who tends to ruminate about problems, realize that your mind will be concerned and your body will react. Like any trauma, these reactions are going to be something that you have to work through for a while.

Oddly enough, taking such a perspective helps the trauma to pass more quickly. Knowing that you are going through a process helps you to take a more detached perspective with respect to it. Although you may experience your body becoming tense, and feel powerless to do anything about it, you also know that this feeling will pass with time.

After the initial trauma, realize that you are going to go through a healing process. This is a time when you begin to recover from the shock of whatever happened to you and can then go through a healing process. Although many injuries heal with time, you can help the healing process by engaging in such activities as prayer or by distracting your mind so that you can take a rest from the event.

One aspect of worry that we have not discussed thus far is that of the impact that unfortunate events can have upon spiritual growth. When bad things happen to us, they do present us with the possibility of learning to be more compassionate. Many Buddhist writers today, most notably Pema Chodron, are popularizing this idea. Books such as *Start Where You Are* and *When Things Fall Apart* teach the importance of suffering as a means to becoming more compassionate.

In our own tradition we know that suffering has its place. We know that Saint Paul suffered from his thorn so that God may be glorified. And we know that Jesus, whom we are to imitate, suffered and died for our sins. There is the opportunity for sanctification through suffering; that is, for experiencing God's kingdom to a greater degree while helping others experience this kingdom.

The problem is that many people seek religion and spirituality as a means of escaping from suffering. They hope that in praying they will be spared from the results of an unfortunate event. And sometimes they are. Yet, in the end, it is all about getting closer to God. God, in his wisdom, realizes that sometimes we must suffer in order to be presented with the opportunity of loving him and loving our neighbors to a greater degree. While this certainly doesn't do much as far as explaining why there is suffering in the world, it does provide us with a spiritual response to it. It is one, I believe, that reaches to the Scriptures. When Jesus saw suffering, he did something about it.

I don't want to pass this off as an easy thing to do, however. When something bad happens, we want to be spared from it. If we aren't spared we become afraid and feel that we are all alone in dealing with it. Frequently, too, we feel guilty, or perhaps stigmatized, by the event. We feel alone in our pain, miserable, guilty, and afraid. Again, it helps to realize that this is a process you must go through. It doesn't do much good to berate yourself by saying that if you were more spiritual this wouldn't have happened to you. It also doesn't help to say that if you were a better person you would handle the event better and it wouldn't bother you so much. Instead, allow yourself to go through the process, realizing that at some point you will be able to find opportunities to turn the event into a means of spiritual growth and compassion.

Love and Silence

I'd like to talk about one particular area of suffering because it is one that I face quite a bit, and one that is troubling to many. This has to do with dealing with the many difficult people that one faces in life. Such people cause a lot of pain and anxiety through the words that they say and the actions that they take. These people are hard to handle from a Christian perspective. We are taught to love our neighbors as ourselves and to turn the other cheek. Yet loving these people is difficult and turning the other cheek sometimes makes them strike the other cheek even harder (speaking figuratively, of course).

I remember a story one clergyman told me about his experiences visiting the poet Andrew Lytle up on Mount Eagle in Tennessee. "You're either about love or power," he would say. People more interested in power will act a certain way. They will be less concerned about the people they interact with and more concerned with whatever they are trying to gain or accomplish. People more interested in love are more concerned with how they can help others. Needless to say, the people who are interested in power tend to step on the toes of those who are interested in love. For those interested in love, it helps to remember Lytle's saying. It helps to see where the power-centered individual is coming from. It can also deflect some of the pain caused by such individuals. You can see the game that this person is playing. This helps to silence the voice inside of you that is telling you that you have been wronged. It also silences the internal voice that is also interested in power (and we all have that voice). What you may be able to do in thinking about this saying is to take an attitude that is centered on love. In doing this, your response will focus upon what is best for you and for others, and may even help you to take a more loving stance toward the power-centered individual (who may well be on the path to becoming your enemy). It's not that you have to be a doormat for such a person. It's more that you consider how your responses further God's kingdom. If such a person is causing harm to you or to others, and you can do something about it, you will do it. If no immediate action is readily available, you will at least not allow the actions of this individual to poison your mind with hatred. It's all about love or power, and you want to chose love.

Effectively dealing with life's events means practicing silence in some instances and practicing selective internal dialogue in others. When you talk to yourself, consider whether your words are coming from a center of power or from a center of love. It also means understanding you aren't in control of all that happens to you. You are going to make mistakes, and people and things are going to come along that work against you.

Remembering Gandhi's advice to be the change you would like to see in the world is helpful here. This gets you away from feeling like a victim and helps you to take positive action. When some person or some event comes along and causes you pain, it is easy to withdraw or to become bitter. Yet it is likely that such a person or event is working against a larger change you would like to see in the world. Perhaps you would like people to be kinder, or you would like the world to be a better place. Yet along comes something or someone that seems to perpetuate anger or anguish. Instead of reacting negatively against an event, you can take positive measures. You can decide to practice compassion, even when the world is confronting you with a lack of compassion. The small steps that you take will have beneficial consequences, even if you don't always see them.

One of the greatest examples of this kind of attitude is found within the pages of Corrie ten Boom's *The Hiding Place*. Here you will find the true story of Corrie's sister Betsie. Both Betsie and Corrie were captured by the Germans during World War II. The entire family was working in the German resistance in Holland, trying to transport Jews safely out of the country. Although Betsie and Corrie endured innumerable hardships in Nazi prisons, Betsie especially never let the cruelty she encountered turn her into an angry or bitter person. Instead, she looked upon even her captors with compassion. In an outlook that is at times stunning, she felt sorry for the guards who were torturers. She was sorry that they had gotten into a state where they had lost their personhood, and told her sister that they had to do something for them if they ever got out of the camp. Corrie did survive the war, while Betsie died in prison before the war ended. Betsie's compassion resonated with Corrie long after the War. Corrie did do much for the victims of the war, both for the torturers and the tortured.

The example of Betsie ten Boom is clear. When faced with the difficulties of life, difficulties which can be tragic and horrendous, you can still be the change you would like to see in the world. You can still act with compassion. That compassion makes a difference, even if its consequences won't be experienced until after your lifetime.

Of course, you don't have to wait for negative experiences in order to be the change you would like to see in the world. You can start by simply thinking about what you would like to see the world to be like. How would you like people to act toward one another? What would people do in a better world? Maybe they would be more tolerant of one another's imperfections. Maybe they wouldn't let things get under their skin so much. Perhaps they would help one another more. When you have a good idea of what qualities in people would bring about a better world, try to embody those qualities in your own life.

Skillful Living

An important idea in this is to think of your efforts as something of a skill that you are developing. This idea is one that is developed in Gregory Jones' *Embodying Forgiveness*. Jones sees forgiveness as a craft and that Christians should try to become proficient at this craft. This is part of building God's kingdom. This is true of practically any virtue, as well as any attempt to embody a positive change in the world. Like any skill, you may not be particularly good at reacting positively to situations at first. As you try to be the change that you would like to see in the world, something is likely to come along that will knock you down. It may even be a small thing. It might be that you hear someone has made a negative comment against you and you respond in kind, forgetting to show the kind of compassion that you would like to see in the world. Or it might be that you simply don't get your way on an issue, and you allow that to cause you to complain a great deal.

Thinking of your efforts as a skill, you can recover from such negative responses and learn to react better. Take an objective look at yourself and your actions, and give yourself credit when you are successful at the craft of kindness. Realize when you have furthered the kingdom of God.

This last point brings us to the change that we, as Christians, should be trying to embody. This is that of participating in the extension of the God's kingdom. This kingdom is comprised of compassion. We are all craftspeople on this journey, trying to put into practice skills in line with this kingdom. There are several skills that go along with this, skills such as forgiveness, compassion, kindness, and love. They are the tools of the trade in which we are called to participate.

Is silence part of this craft? Interior silence is helpful in several ways. It creates the space in us to commune with God and the Holy Spirit. This is an invaluable source of inspiration and comfort in a troubled world. Without this aid, we would not be able to practice the craft. Moreover, interior silence allows us to get beyond the slings and arrows that the world casts in our direction. We can stop the cycle of anger that keeps us from practicing compassion. Learning how to stop the negative talk in our brains is enormously helpful in this regard. Finally, learning through silence to stop engaging in negative conversations with others is helpful as we act in the world. We can begin to control the amount of negative energy we put out. We can learn to stop engaging in the negative conversations of the world, conversations that do a great deal of harm. We can silence those conversations and look for opportunities to practice compassion in our speech and in our actions.

One thing you can do is to find people who exemplify good action and speech. Look for people around you who exude a kind of saintly quality in their ordinary life. Such people can be great teachers, even if they don't know that they are teaching. You can observe the way they treat those who come to them seeking advice. Look at how they handle tough situations when they come along. See how they go through a typical day. Learn from the conversations that they engage in, as well as those in which they don't participate. Such people often teach very simple but powerful lessons as they go through the day.

Another activity you can undertake is to find a community where you can share your struggles as you attempt to make silence and good actions a part of your life. It is enormously helpful if you can find a group of people, perhaps as small as three or four, where you can share with one another the struggles and joy of leading a better life. It is also helpful to include some diversity in your group, perhaps by looking for people from different backgrounds or simply people who work in different places. That way you will be challenged to explain the background conditions that you face in terms that everyone can understand. This exercise in and of itself often provides insight. Moreover, you will benefit from the thoughts and opinions of "outsiders." This can give you a fresh perspective on the situation. I have found such groups to be extremely helpful in working through situations I have faced. It is also a great feeling to provide your own insights to problems that others face. In all of this, it is simply a wonderful and supportive experience to have an environment of friends sharing with one another.

I believe that as a spiritual discipline, silence offers a great deal to those who seek it. It is through silence that we often find God. The mystical experience of God is one that is often hard to put into words. Our words simply cannot grasp that which is in many respects beyond comprehension. We can carry over this experience and this silence to our daily life. We can learn to include silence in our prayer life, as well as in our interactions with others. We can learn to silence ourselves when we start to say an unkind word. We can learn to silence ourselves when we know we are about to engage in a conversation that is going to create ill will. We can find ways to seek silence when we are around people who are engaging in unfortunate conversations. And we can learn to be silent within ourselves, practicing a deep reverence in our internal dialogue.

My experience at the Abbey of Gethsemane was one in which a sense of joy became part of my being. This is a sense that is hard to explain, hard to put into words. Learning to be silent helps to clear the path to such an experience of God. It helps to stop the senseless, often defensive chatter that goes through my brain during the day. The paradox is that it is only through silence that we are filled. When we learn to empty ourselves of all the worries and fears that go along with living in the modern world, we can allow ourselves to be filled with the love of God. This is a stressful world in which we live. There is always some reason to feel that you aren't measuring up, that you've made a mistake, or that your effort isn't worthy. To live successfully and joyfully we have to get beyond such thinking. The way to this isn't still more self-criticism for being so weak as to engage in such behavior. The way to this is to find the silent self. Learn to silence your worries as much as you can. Learn to take action, and then move on. Learn to be tolerant of yourself and others. Learn to deal with those people who aren't tolerant. Keep such people from forming a dialogue against you in your own mind. Empty yourself

so that you can be filled. Be silent so you can hear God.
Make that your spiritual practice.

TEN

Practicing Joy

J ust as a great deal has happened in my life since that spring day on the grounds of the Abbey of Gethsemane, a lot has happened in the year since I started writing this book. I have dealt with family illnesses and setbacks, as well as the usual stresses and strains of having a full-time job. I have also enjoyed good friendships, as well as personal and professional successes. As I moved through this year, I tried to apply the ideas of this book. At times I did this well and was able to take things in stride. At other times I didn't take things well and was overtaken by fear and fatigue.

The questions raised by this book are practical ones. How can you apply the ideas found here in a fast-paced, troubled world such as our own? This challenge is found within the very title of this chapter. "Practicing joy" sounds like an oxymoron. How can you practice something that often seems spontaneous? Joy is a fleeting experience, something that seems more a gift than the result of a discipline. The same can be said of my experience at the Abbey of Gethsemane. Wasn't that experience really a grace, something given by God, rather than something I earned through years of hard work? Am I wrong in suggesting that following three disciplines is a way to attain something that is really freely and, perhaps, mysteriously given by God?

Being a human being means to be inclined in certain directions. Unfortunately this means being inclined to take one's self too seriously. It also means being inclined to sin. Turning away from God, which is really what we do when we focus on ourselves, cuts us off from God's grace and joy. Disciplines are a way of connecting to this grace and joy. I believe that's what Jesus was trying to tell us in the Sermon on the Mount. Stop focusing on yourself and start focusing on the love of God.

Altering this focus is a difficult business. That's why I believe that the disciplines mentioned in this book are necessary. Without them we are likely to continue to be concerned with who we are, what we are getting out of life, and how circumstances may either help or harm us.

I know from experience, however, that attempting to practice more than one discipline can be especially hard. Just when you think you are making progress in humility, you find yourself facing some complicating factor that gets in the way of simplicity. Or, just as you feel you have simplified your life, you find yourself forsaking silence so that you can talk excessively about your simplification efforts to others.

Is there a good way of putting these disciplines together into an effective practice? Does doing so really create a greater sense of joy? Let's take a look at these two questions separately. The difficulty of progressing in the spiritual life is literally the stuff of legends. Joseph Campbell and others have made careers exploring how the myths of various cultures connect to progress upon the spiritual path. Connecting this in turn to my own life over the past year, it is easy to see how difficult this task is. It's hard to stay focused on God and to practice God's presence when you are in situations where your judgment can be questioned or where events can overtake you. It's also hard to make progress when you have to overcome desires to be secure and to be loved, adored, and respected. It's easy to feel like King Arthur's Knights seeking the elusive Holy Grail. You feel you are never quite good enough to attain it.

It helps to remember that such disciplines as those mentioned in this book are in fact helpers to a holier life. Without them, you may feel doomed to forever seeking an unattainable goal. With them, you now have the means to remove the obstacles in your path to joy.

I have already provided pointers on how to practice humility, simplicity, and silence in the chapters that deal with these topics. One simple way of putting these ideas together is to ask a single question with respect to each. How am I doing in my practice of humility? How am I doing in my practice of simplicity? How am I doing in my practice of silence? Answering each of these questions will help you to get a quick assessment of your progress.

Looking at how you are doing with your practice of humility means focusing on how seriously you are taking yourself. Do you see yourself as the center of the universe? Are you trying to make things bend to your will rather than seeking the will of God? On a more difficult and penetrating level, are you trying to create an understanding of God's will so that it justifies your position or your actions?

One way of assessing your practice of humility is whether you are letting go. Letting go means letting go of the excessive worries that tend to dominate people in the modern world. This may be followed up with thinking about how much you are serving others. Humility calls us to help others. This can be done grudgingly out of a sense of duty or lovingly out of a sense of the worth of other people. Are you finding both large and small ways to help people where you work as well as in the community? Do you let cynicism and fatigue keep you from acts of beneficence?

Based upon my own experience and those of the people around me, simplicity is really a never-ending struggle. You have to work at simplifying your life. You have to work at finding ways to deal with the junk mail, the telephone solicitors, and the other uncalled for little intrusions that come into your life. You also have to refrain from taking on too much responsibility and from having to keep an all-too-demanding world at bay.

Everyday I face people who have seemingly given into the complicating factors of life. These are people who work so hard that they fail to do such basic things as exercise regularly, get enough sleep, and eat healthily. In many respects, these people are working themselves to death. They may be doing this for noble reasons, but they are doing this nonetheless.

Simplicity requires effort. But once the effort has been expended, you should see some payoffs fairly quickly. You will know that your life is simpler when your pace is less hectic and when you have time for the things that really matter to you. Conversely, you know that your life is too complicated when you feel worn out at the end of the day, and when you feel that you have really accomplished nothing of significance and importance to you. When you get to that point, simply take a few minutes to readjust your life.

How do you know if you have enough silence in your life? This is a matter of looking at both social and internal dialogue. You are making too much noise if you find yourself getting into constant conflicts with people or if you are saying things that are really not of much consequence or importance whatsoever. Gossip, making jokes at the expense of others, and generally hurtful comments are also an indication of too much noise.

You know that you are doing better with interior silence if you are not engaged in a lot of self-recrimination. Rather than focusing on yourself and either your ability or inability to attain perfection, you are focused upon service to God and others. Just as the quotes from Frederick Beuchner and Brother David Steindl-Rast indicated in chapter 1, there is a sense of not focusing on yourself here. In Beuchner's terms, you aren't focusing on yourself at all. In Steindl-Rast's terms, you are emptying yourself so that you can be filled.

As is true of simplicity, your energy level may be a good indicator of how you are doing with silence. Fatigue can mean that you are spending a lot of time defending yourself or engaged in idle talk. It can also result from spending a lot of time engaged in negative internal dialogue. You can gently push yourself away from such negative chatter. The result is often a sense of calm and peace.

Putting these disciplines together means going through the brief exercise of asking how you are doing with each one. Once you do that, you are likely to see that they are really very connected. I tend to think of humility as being the core discipline of the three. If you are living humbly, then you are likely also to be doing well with simplicity and with silence. You aren't trying to complicate your life with goods and possessions, just as you aren't trying to fill the world with your knowledge and intelligence on every last issue. Humility is the key.

But how do all of these disciplines combine to lead to joy? That's very simple. When you stop being so concerned about yourself, then you can let go of the things that are stressful to you. Buddhists say that the way to get past suffering is to do something about your desire. If you can stop your desire for something, no matter what that something may be, then your suffering will go away. Christians have a slightly different path with respect to this. If you can die to yourself, then you are free to take on Christ and to imitate him. This, too, does something with your desire. In desiring Christ, you stop the endless chase of things that don't really matter. The blessing in this is that there is a great deal of joy involved in this. Your burden is lighter, and your heart is filled with peace.

Of course, in many respects, it is hard for others in the world to understand this process. Others may feel that you aren't being serious enough, or that you aren't giving enough to the cause, whatever the cause may be. You will be condemned for being too much of a lightweight. To combat this way of thinking, take a look around you. Who are the happy and blissful people in your world? Are they the ambitious ones, who lead complicated lives full of storm and movement? Or are they the ones focused in their own quiet way upon God? Time after time, I have found that such people are in the latter category. There must be something to that.

I began this book by talking about my experience at the Abbey of Gethsemane. There the prayers of others, prayers that hadn't even been made yet, lifted my spirits and allowed me to experience the closeness of God. I believe that closeness is always there. Returning to that experience, and the joy that goes along with it, requires that I learn to be more open to it, and be more open to God. Humility, simplicity, and silence are disciplines that allow me to do this.

But, in the end, do they work? I can only speak from my own experience. The fact for me is that they do. I know when I am taking myself too seriously. It's when I no longer experience God and the joy that God brings. I know I get back to this joy when, in humility, simplicity, and silence, I learn to love and serve God and to love and serve my neighbor. Like all disciplines, it takes time to get better at them, so I can't say that I am anywhere near perfect in my practice. I expect these are disciplines that take a lifetime to achieve something like mastery. But I know it's possible, because I have seen it done so many times by people around me.

Joy is something that must be practiced in the modern world. There is so much to be concerned about and so many tragedies that take place around us. While you shouldn't blind yourself to these events, there is something to be said for focusing on God and allowing God to guide your reactions to the personal and the planetary. In doing this, you will find moments of peace where you can think clearly and where you feel connected to something beyond your immediate surroundings. You can use this connection to bring this peace and joy to others.

My experience at Gethsemane was not so much of an earth-shattering change as it was a subtle reminder of what connectedness to God feels like. As a concluding exercise to this book, I encourage you to think of a time or times when you felt a particularly closeness to God. What was this like? What was the circumstance in which it took place? Are there particular disciplines that you can identify that may create this sense of closeness again?

It is my belief that though at times difficult and "countercultural," humility, simplicity, and silence are parts of a direct pathway to God. They are means by which you focus less upon yourself and more on God. A final test of this is to remember this at times when you are particularly stressed or troubled. In humility, turn to God and offer your thoughts to God. Many times you will find that while the circumstances may not change, your reaction to them will. You will discover the great joy that God has to offer no matter what the circumstances.

But while remembering that this joy is freely given, also remember that, as humans, we have to work at experiencing it. For that we have the endless virtues of humility, simplicity, and silence. These are worthy tools for the craft of experiencing an endless love for an endless God.